IN
ANOTHER
WORLD

By Gerald Dawe

Poetry

Sheltering Places

The Lundys Letter

Sunday School

Heart of Hearts

The Morning Train

Lake Geneva

Points West

Selected Poems

Mickey Finn's Air

Early Poems

❖

*The Night Fountain: Selected Early Poems
of Salvatore Quasimodo* (with Marco Sonzogni)

❖

Prose

The Proper Word: Collected Criticism

The Lagan Series: 2007–2015

*Of War and War's Alarms: Reflections on Modern Irish
Writing*

❖

Editor

The Younger Irish Poets

The New Younger Irish Poets

*Earth Voices Whispering: An Anthology of Irish War
Poetry 1914–1945*

The Cambridge Companion to Irish Poets

GERALD DAWE

IN ANOTHER WORLD

Van Morrison & Belfast

MERRION
PRESS

First published in 2017 by
Merrion Press
10 George's Street
Newbridge
Co. Kildare
Ireland
www.merrionpress.ie

9781785371462 (Cloth)
9781785371516 (Kindle)
9781785371523 (Epub)
9781785371530 (PDF)

British Library Cataloguing in Publication Data
An entry can be found on request

Library of Congress Cataloging in Publication Data
An entry can be found on request

Interior design: Sin É Design
Typeset: Sabon 11/15 pt

Cover photograph: Margaret Lonergan
Cover design: edit+ and Margaret Lonergan,
www.stuartcoughlan.com

Serious, often grave, but inculcated with such sympathy and passion and affection that any obscurity is the enemy. It's as if what Gerald Dawe has to tell us is so vital that clarity – such a virtue – is a moral matter.
–Richard Ford

For Joe and Ellison, Eon and Maria, and the rest of the gang.

CONTENTS

PREFACE xii

ONE 1
TWO 16
THREE 28
FOUR 47
FIVE 67
SIX 80
SEVEN 99

ACKNOWLEDGEMENTS 113

SELECT BIBLIOGRAPHY 114

PREFACE

Belfast in the 1960s was full of music. The city centre had many clubs and dance halls, pubs and 'hops' where an extraordinary variety of music was performed. From traditional Irish music to trad jazz to music hall (the dying embers) to showbands and to the proliferating urban sound of R & B – that rawer, passionate, bluesy encounter that became a signature of the times. Certainly for many of the young generation born in the post-war provincial city, venues such as The Maritime or Sammy Houston's Jazz Club became meccas of dance and live music. Before the curtain dropped in the late 1960s and the city, despite the best efforts of thousands of ordinary men and women who braved the terror, fell into a kind of fragmented darkness, Belfast's vibrant music scene was a liberation.

In record shops like Dougie Knight's, in boutiques like John Patrick's or Dukes, and in clubs like The Maritime (and its successor, Club Rado), you could live in Belfast's city centre and bypass the sectarian bile. People really did get on with it; and get it on. The names of the illustrious blues, rock and R & B artists who played the city during the 1960s are legion, and the respect in which some were held was considerable. When Otis Redding, the great R & B and soul singer, died tragically in December 1967 at the age of twenty-six in a plane crash in Wisconsin, en route to a Sunday evening concert in Madison, young men in Belfast wore black armbands. The former well-driller from Georgia was a kind of icon to many hundreds, maybe thousands, in the provincial Northern city. 'Pain in My Heart', 'Mr Pitiful', 'That's How Strong My Love Is', 'Shake', 'I've Been Loving You Too Long', 'Sad Song', 'Respect' and 'Dock of the Bay' were anthems for a group of young men and women who dressed in imitation of black American 'cool'. In 'night' clubs and in afternoon sessions in Belfast's Plaza, we would dance our young lives away – solo, with our girls, or in groups. It was a macho scene. Fights were not uncommon, though sudden and short-lived; what mattered was something other than 'scrapping'.

White blues on vinyl from Chicago, such as Paul Butterfield; neat, three-piece jazz combos, such as The Peddlers; touring bands under John Mayall, from the Bluesbreakers through Aynsley Dunbar's Retaliation; Cream, Chicken Shack, Fleetwood Mac; black blues men like Champion Jack Dupree; soul and R & B like Gino Washington and the Ram Jam Band, and many other first-rate variations performed regularly in the city throughout the 1960s.

Why there was such an intense appetite for R & B, soul, blues and jazz in a city that became synonymous with the most virulent kind of sectarian violence is a question that has more to do with clichéd perceptions of Belfast than with a rounded appreciation of the city. Had it something to do with the thousands of America's GIs, many of them black, stationed in the North during the Second World War who brought their music with them? Or the human traffic that swept thousands of men and women to America throughout the last century in search of work, particularly in the recessionary years preceding the Second World War? Or perhaps it was due to the more immediate cultural bonds that linked industrial Belfast, the harbour port, to other industrial ports like Liverpool, Glasgow, Newcastle and of course London? Belfast families had for generations moved back and forth across the narrow stretch of the Irish Sea, in their search for work, taking with them an inherited local exposure to music of one kind or another.

Both radio and television, but primarily the former, were a hugely influential and great transmitter of music in the 1950s. The freedom of movement that the transistor radio brought allowed a younger generation to switch channels to the independent radio stations, such as Radio Caroline or Luxembourg, and play 'their own' music, wherever and whenever they wanted, indoors or out, day or night.

By the 1960s, television programmes such as *Ready Steady Go!* and *Six Five Special* were putting faces, styles and dance moves to the music. There were also the weekly musical magazines, including *Melody Maker* and *New Musical Express*.

Was there a widespread, urban elan that R & B, blues and soul represented for a generation of post-war working- and middle-class kids, alongside the increase in general affluence which Belfast had started to experience along with other British cities? I don't know. The music that developed from the city certainly revelled in its self-assured, passionate singing as much as its raw, intimate, emotional energy. Them was one of the more well-known local bands, and Van Morrison, their lead vocalist and guiding spirit, unquestionably gave voice to that mood.

But there was another side to the story – a poetic side to Morrison's achievement that has kept achieving, producing over the next fifty years lyrics of the first order, and some of the best popular love songs of modern times. In the summer of 1970, sitting on the tiny balcony of my mother's flat, which overlooked a square in an estate of houses in east Belfast, I was looking at the sky when 'These Dreams of You' came over the radio; the voice of my home town. This is what *In Another World* is about.

Gerald Dawe
Dún Laoghaire/Belfast
October 2017

ONE

The radio had a cloth face and was quite an imposing-looking object, sitting in an alcove of the living room, alone, slightly iconic, above the television that was equally sturdy-looking in its timber housing. The furniture of the 1950s remains set in place: the sofa, the presses, the dinner table, the side table, the baize tablecloth with its tassels, the little door under the stairs, the stepdown to the foreboding pantry, the workaday cottage-like air of that kitchen, and the yard with its high walls, mangle, washing line, larder, coal sheds, outdoor lavatory and the door to the entry or alleyway.

The back of the house was the working half, the engine room; the front was for entertainment and, in our case, for business – where my grandmother taught elocution, piano and singing. The rest of the house was all about privacy, rest, dreamland.

It was an unexceptional house, in its own little terrace, a version of grander houses with grander expectations, a different kind of lifestyle than had been lived in the earlier decades of the last century. Now, post-war, post-marriages, in this house of women – grandmother, mother and sister – I was the only man (and a mere slip of a boy at that), notwithstanding the occasional visit of my uncle, stationed in foreign climes, and of my grandmother's party-going friends – ageing stylists of a bygone time.

I remember it all well. Or maybe I remember well what I think it all was. One way or another, in the regular world of those years, as people got on with their lives as best they could – the experience of the Blitz still very much inscribed on the Belfast landscape of the time – and returned to a normal world of work and play, I was utterly unaware of all this. As a self-absorbed young boy I was, however, fascinated by stories overheard, the hints of a previous world, before 'my' world, the way things 'once were'; my young-boy radar fixed on the songs that came out of the front room, the laughter, the recitations, the piano playing, the singing, but also the music that 'came over' the box in the corner, and by decade's end, the sound of music my mother listened to, from *Workers' Playtime* to Billy Cotton, *Two-Way Family Favourites,* the Broadway hits, swing and trad jazz. And when her brother was home 'on leave' from the RAF, the sound of American leading ladies, such as the queen-like Ella Fitzgerald, but also the unmissable, alluring otherness of quite a different voice – rich, exciting and unforgettable – Sarah Vaughan, a familiar name, a name you might hear in the street, and yet so totally unexpected. It was probably from listening to my aunt's stories of minding Judy Garland during the fading star's last great hurrah in London's Palladium, as well as her anecdotes about Frank Sinatra and the swooning English girls who fell head over heels in love with the great crooner of the 1950s that sparked my interest.

Our house always had music somewhere – from piano practice to that big awkward radio set that sat brooding in the corner of the living room: Edmundo Ros gave way on the Light Programme to Nat King Cole and Peggy Lee, and by the end of the 1950s and into the early years of the 1960s, the radio yielded to the transistor, and more emphatically to the glumpy record player that took over the front room.

My mother enjoyed jazz. She listened to it on the radio, and when her brother finally left the RAF and settled briefly back in Belfast, he brought records with him. The television, which formed part of our communication centre, sat there under the radio, and between them both the sounds of British jazz started to filter through: Acker Bilk's 'Stranger on the Shore' was a signature tune; Kenny Baker, with his bouncing Brylcreem hairline; George Chisholm, and the cool, perplexing beauty of Cleo Laine's voice, with Johnny Dankworth, a seemingly shy presence in the shadowy background of whatever show it was we were watching.

Laine sounded so different, when compared to other acts that were beginning to get air time, at that moment with singers such as Helen Shapiro and Dusty Springfield. There was something so utterly contained in her voice that even when she went off on one of those scat-like *a cappella* riffs – part madrigal, pure invention – I wasn't sure what to make of it. The calm seriousness, the conviction, the controlled flights of invention – for a young lad, it was all breathtakingly uncertain what was going on.

There was a jazz combo I used to love hearing called The Peddlers, and on one show on which they were guests (when they performed a brilliant version of 'Misty'), Cleo Laine appeared after their set. The mood she created on our black-and-white TV was haunting and mysterious.

When the chance arose many years later, during the Belfast Festival at Queen's University, I went along to hear Cleo Laine and Johnny Dankworth talk about their music and play extracts of it. I think it was in the old Music Room, one of the smaller lecture theatres, and there were about twenty people present. That's what it seems like in memory, at least; I recall my discomfort at being one of a few and not really knowing where to look; but they talked and joked and we had a session, unplugged before unplugged happened. I'll never forget that. This is what real artists do, I thought; the *size* of the audience isn't important.

Looking out the back window, waiting for *Match of the Day* or *The Day of the Triffids* to come blinking on to the television set in the gathering dusk of a Saturday night, a young lad born in the early 1950s hears for the first time Sarah Vaughan sing her great love song 'Lover Man', and the 1960s break cover in north Belfast.

What stands out in my mind is that house in which we lived in north Belfast throughout the late 1950s and into the 1960s. It overlooked the lough and harbour port. My grandmother was a singer, a light-opera singer, and she used to have these soirées in the front room. I used to stand at the top of the stairs listening to this, and it always fascinated me that it was as if there was a little theatre in the front room.

It was always very well organised, it was good fun and the pupils enjoyed themselves; they would always leave happy. What struck me from an early age (I would have been five or six at the time) about the adult soirées she held at night, and at weekends, was their manner. Everything was contained – nothing ever got out of hand, and even though the people enjoyed themselves and you could hear the laughter, there was something reserved about it all. My grandmother would sing the odd time, but mostly she kept her voice to herself, so to speak.

Later on, with the record player in the front room, my sister and I took over that space and I'd play records by people like Lester Young, George Shearing and Ella Fitzgerald. I used to hear Ella on that gramophone: another woman's voice to join the voices of the women I lived with. And then one night, Ella Fitzgerald played Belfast. I remember my mother coming back from it – she went to that 'gig' with our next-door neighbour, an Austrian woman – and she was very excited and told me it had been an extraordinary experience.

The funny little comment that she made, 'I'm sent' stuck in my mind – clearly she was rocking and rolling in the aisles, not literally, but almost. Our next-door neighbour was rather austere about such displays. She was a private woman who had endured a lot during the Second World War in Vienna, where she had met her husband, one of the liberating Allied officers. My mother's enthusiasm for this music was infectious. What I remember most about those days was a feeling of being underground, though I'm sure there were other houses throughout Belfast where this kind of interest in music was being shown in the parlours and living rooms.

There must have been an adult generation who had done something similar a decade *before* the 1950s, when all the soldiers had returned from the war. There is an obvious parallel. They had been stationed in Germany, listening to American music, and there had been a whole series of army installations in Northern Ireland. Black guys stationed there must have been playing music. They'd go down to the Plaza Ballroom in Belfast; they'd have been dancing down there too.

There were so many different kinds of music at that time, but the one that seemed to have the biggest impact was jazz, in all its subversiveness. By the early 1960s, a group of little clubs springing up around the town were playing R & B, soul and Tamla Motown. A bridge was built between the likes of Ella Fitzgerald and Lester Young, whom I was hearing in the late 1950s, and then, ten years later, with the friends I had in my mid-teens, we started to get into R & B and blues.

The one voice, the one name that summed all that up for us was Van Morrison and Them. There were other very good bands around during the mid-sixties, like The Few, The Interns, Sam Mahood and The Just

Five. It seemed there were bands playing every night. I remember clearly that we didn't get into the pop stuff so much as young teenagers. It was mainly R & B and then acts like the Jimi Hendrix Experience that were popular with us.

Belfast was still open then. Everybody lived in the city and there wasn't a sense that the city was ghettoised or that there were neighbourhoods you couldn't move in and out of; the city centre was a home for everybody and it had a marvellous energy to it. There would be dances on a Wednesday night, Friday night, Saturday afternoon, Saturday night, and even Sunday. Everybody went dancing. Around the side of the City Hall, one afternoon in late spring, the weather was good and somebody had a transistor on. We were lying on the grass and we heard Van Morrison with Them, singing 'Here Comes the Night'. That song became a theme tune, a hymn.

When I started to go to The Maritime (where Them had played), it had changed its name and was called Club Rado, although we all still knew it by its original name. I never saw Them live on stage, though I did hear Morrison on the tiny stage of Sammy Houston's Jazz Club performing Dylan's 'Like A Rolling Stone' with Frankie Connolly and the Styx, a rare combination for sure.

What I do recall very clearly is the energy in Van Morrison's voice, a very Belfast voice. That somebody could get up on stage and sing with the accent you heard in the streets was unimaginable. To think that this was a guy from Belfast who was on *Ready Steady*

Go!, a guy who was in a band that was doing well in Britain, and, despite all this, you'd see him around town the odd time. It was a great source of pride.

In those days there wasn't the hype or the self-consciousness that there is today. Them with Van Morrison gave voice to a generation. I don't want to put too much on it, but we did not know a great deal about sectarianism. It just wasn't part of the psychic landscape. I used to date girls from the top of the Falls Road and we'd walk home together. We used to walk everywhere. Everybody used to meet in the clubs; Van captured that defiance in his voice and, with Them, aggressively declared 'We're here', with a kind of dismissiveness, publicly, about being in 'the business'– the music business. I know now that they had to fight their corner.

I can imagine some would have been badly treated by 'the industry', but Morrison stood for a kind of independence. We wouldn't have been conscious of this at the time, but there was certainly the sense in which he was doing his thing and then just moving on. It wasn't as if he was being a 'pop star' – that wasn't there at all. This music was something he could 'do', something he was brilliant at. He'd get on stage with the band and then go. In a way, he was an anti-hero. Them were anti-heroes and they fitted the mood. But it wouldn't have been a conscious thing, a pose. Morrison went on to become more sophisticated.

We tried different things and in Smithfield – which was a market, like a casbah – you could buy and sell just about anything, including records, second-hand records. It was magnificent – coins, clothes, old transistor radios, wardrobes, you name it – and there was one shop, the name of which won't come to mind now, and the fella who had this shop was very interested in music, soul, R & B and blues.

I will never forget going into that shop. To see this guy, you'd think he should be looking under the bonnet of a car, but when he started to talk about blues and R & B, you were in another world. He knew everything: different versions of the same songs – exactly who was who in the States. We used to go in and talk and I remember one time he put on a track – it was a Chess album track of John Lee Hooker. We were all in the shop (it was just a big counter and the records were stacked behind it), and it was extraordinary to hear this guy.

There was the feeling then that music was the counter-culture. Belfast was very much a city dominated by work – that is what you were there for – work, work, work.

When I think of the 1960s, people's energies were directed at getting out and about; getting into Belfast. Them, the Belfast band that was doing so well, personified this feeling of being able to express yourself 'here'. They suggested to those of us who were about six or seven years younger that you could do these things, that you needn't be afraid to set up your own band. We did; just that and we called our band The Trolls.

We played in different places. We were pretty desperate. I think we lasted about six months and that was it. But it was the kind of confidence Them gave myself and a few others I knew which made me start to write. We realised we weren't singers, we weren't musicians, but we could move into other 'art forms'.

In that sense, Van Morrison opened the door for myself and other young men and women to think that 'work' wasn't the only way forward, that there was a different kind of work and you could do it on the stage or with a pen. It was the possibilities Them generated that were so important. They broke the sound barriers of what was often an uptight, class-bound society. By the late 1960s, when Them had broken up, Van Morrison was really on his way out because he'd gone over to the States. We lost sight of him, but then he produced the album that everybody recognises and identifies as being so extraordinary – *Astral Weeks*. The thing to remember is that Belfast was on the cusp of a whole series of changes. The Civil Rights movement was up and going.

A lot of friends had left Belfast and were now in London or had disappeared elsewhere. When *Astral Weeks* came out, there were just a few of us still around. To listen to that album, which was a huge poetic shift away from the raucous energies of Them, and pointed in another direction too – towards poetry. For the mood poem that is *Astral Weeks* – I mean the entire album, but particularly 'Beside You' – was so revealing. Here was this strong voice and strong personality that could also move across into something so much more lyrical and moody. That was a big shift too. You can be a Belfast guy and you can still be lyrical.

It seems silly now, but the extent to which Morrison had moved into another mode, another mood, shocked people. Then, of course, the curtain fell with the beginning of the Troubles and by about 1970 it seemed as if *Astral Weeks*, Them and all that were light years away.

My feeling now is that Morrison's music 'disappeared' because the immediacy of what was happening in Belfast (the terrorism, the darkness) overtook us. We seemed to lose out; the 'gang' drifted apart; we went our different ways. I went to college in Coleraine and then eventually moved out of the North altogether, to Galway.

The joy, the pleasure and the energy that Morrison embodied went underground as the heavy political charge of the 1970s took over. It was only later that I heard 'Listen to the Lion' from the magnificent *It's Too Late to Stop Now*, a double album of his tour with the Caledonian Soul Orchestra. What you had was an artist who could lift the roof and bring together these different forms of music. You had the energy of the voice, the dynamic quality of it, and that marked an entire period for me. That was Van Morrison, doing his thing and not being compromised by 'pop'. You had the feeling that he was going to produce something quite different.

We had a strong sense of being from Belfast. We didn't really have a sense of being 'Irish' as such. When you think about it, great bands used to come to Belfast – John Mayall, Hendrix, Cream, The Small Faces and Pink Floyd. We didn't have to go to them. In a way, we were almost arrogant about music. The standards we were used to were phenomenal, so it created the expectation that everything else had to measure up. We really had such a marvellous experience in Belfast. Occasionally you'd get some old fella shouting something at you, and there was always a little bit of tension on the periphery, but we had a wonderful time and it lasted until about 1970 – the dancing, the music, the parties, being able to move throughout Belfast freely. By 1972, that had gone, more or less. When I returned home from Galway, the music seemed to have disappeared underground. It felt like we were old men talking about a period thirty years before, rather than only a few years before. There had definitely been a shift.

The Troubles put into quarantine those kinds of energies, but maybe they are resurfacing now. I don't know. I can't stress enough the importance of Morrison's presence in the clubs and the kind of example he set when he moved away from Belfast. I think he ran out of space in Belfast. He'd done all he wanted to do there and he had to go somewhere else.

Perhaps it's not sufficiently recognised that it was a huge step for someone to take in those days – a tremendously courageous thing to do – to move from Belfast and head over to New York, not knowing what was going to happen. That was a remarkable achievement. It's okay now, moving here, there and everywhere; there are huge resources available now. But in 1966, 1967, 1968, that was a big achievement, and of course it paid off, because without the move you probably wouldn't have had *Astral Weeks*. He had been writing some of those lyrics in Belfast, but you wouldn't have had the quality of that magnificent album without the shift and the risk of moving to America and the taking-on of extraordinary responsibilities for such a young man. By the late 1970s there were other clubs in the districts, in local neighbourhoods where people went, but the notion of Belfast itself as open and available had gone. The violence had put paid to that. I remember walking through the city one night – it would've been about 1972 or 1973 – and it was like walking through a ghost town. We're forgetting these things and maybe it's no bad thing. The pubs shut at about 6 or 7pm, the cinemas were closed and the buses stopped early. It was like walking through a city at war with itself. People withdrew into their own districts and then, inside their own districts, back into their own homes; they didn't look out. It was bleak.

During the 1980s, I'd been writing poems in Galway. I remember the sense that I wanted to write about where I'd come from, but I wasn't too sure how to go about it. Then Morrison's example kicked in very strongly. The fact that he'd written about the places, streets and avenues of Belfast that I myself knew helped me. It was as if a light went on and I found myself writing a whole sequence of poems about Belfast. I probably wouldn't have written those without Van Morrison, who had made it possible to write about his own place. It's difficult to think now about the extent to which Belfast had been perceived as being 'anti-art', that you couldn't write poems out of that place. Yet here was this guy who was singing songs and making music, hymns to the Belfast that I knew well.

I published *The Lundys Letter* (1985), and in that there are a number of poems about Belfast and its environs. I think it's very much down to Van Morrison's example, along with one or two poets whose work I greatly admired, namely Derek Mahon and Michael Longley. What strikes me about his music and influence is his ability to move in and out of different forms. He tapped into a form of expression which drew on poets like William Blake, and at the same time brought together some of the American Beat poets. There's a freedom in what he does, and that's exhilarating for a poet. We can get stuck on very narrow gauges, but Morrison's ability to blend, mix and draw on different kinds of energy and generate writing out of his own self was 'empowering', as they say. It was enabling and striking.

Towards the end of the 1980s, Van Morrison was planning a programme on poetry and music and I was involved. We travelled around east Belfast, going to Orangefield – the school that both Van and I had attended. Being with him around that almost 'sacred' environment – the streams, the mountains, the hillside, the whole area – was exciting. I also realised the extent to which he was an artist who had a strong commitment to the place, but also to a particular vision. It wasn't as if he was just documenting this area. He had a powerful sense of how ordinary life is suffused with the spirit of place and, besides the fun that we had, it was intriguing to be with him as he walked through this neighbourhood that he had done so much to praise in his music. Van Morrison's voice is distinct and unique. It's like having a presence that is unmovable. And that's refreshing in this day and age, when people market themselves and put themselves into little slots and niches. Morrison is himself; he does exactly what he wants to do and he's totally committed to that.

The sense you had in Belfast in the 1950s was that everybody had to be in his or her own place; everything was correct; things were in their spot. Music was the way to break out of that; there was a strong feeling that you could escape that control. This was what I loved about it. By the mid-1960s, Van Morrison, Them and others were breaking through and transgressing, just by the sheer energy of their voices and music. Van Morrison's music will live for ever. There are so many magnificent albums, from *Astral Weeks* to the present. Morrison's music will always 'be there' for one basic reason – that he sets out on a journey and he makes a bold statement. The music is not constrained. You can move backwards and forwards through all these different artistic forms: that's an important lesson, and a fantastic example for future generations.

TWO

Coming into Belfast is like approaching a sunken city. It lies inside a horseshoe of surrounding hills; the coastal land to its southern shoreline is the rich, undulating landscape of County Down; on Belfast's northerly shores is County Antrim: a harsher, more dramatic terrain that faces Scotland across the narrow straits of the Sea of Moyle.

Unlike most Irish cities, which give their name to the immediate hinterland – Dublin, Galway, Cork, Sligo, Waterford, Derry, Donegal – Belfast is just itself. The lough at whose mouth the city fans out is fed by the River Lagan, which flows down through the untouched meadows and park forests, along the embankments and under the bridges that link the south and east of the city with the north and west.

In the building docks and islands, old quays and wharves, Belfast's industrial history as a shipbuilding and merchant port makes way for the new ferry terminals. Channels such as Victoria and Musgrave and basins like Pollock, which had borne tankers, liners and gunships for the British fleet, rub shoulders now with a busy and expanding city airport. The massive gantries of the Harland and Wolff shipbuilders

– once the greatest of its kind in the world – straddle the city's horizon like monumental arches.

Clutched around Belfast's inner reaches are the refitted mills and factories, warehouses and engineering works that are isolated by the svelte dominance of motorways and bypasses. What remains of Belfast's industrial architecture has a strangely marooned look to it. The red-brick Gothic of insurance houses and banks, stores and churches, hotels and theatres, which were once the city's Victorian legacy, have all but vanished.

Belfast suffered the fate of many cities in Britain and Ireland caught up in and mauled by the hectic redevelopment boom of the 1980s. What has taken over, inside-out as it were, are the shopping malls, the steel-framed centre and the masked facades. These changes belie another truth, however, of the profound, irrevocable change Belfast experienced as the site of sectarian violence that took possession of the city from the late 1960s: bombing campaigns in the name of Irish national liberation vied with bombing campaigns in the name of preserving the British way of life. Peace lines of metal girders divided communities against themselves; security barriers defaced the cityscape and turned the centre into a police zone during the worst years of the Troubles. The map of the city is a history of territorial allegiances and tribal loyalties.

For anyone growing up in the Belfast of the late 1940s and 1950s, there was always going to be an inbred sense of *where* one walked. This sense of place has been grotesquely theatricalised as a result of the

Troubles and the physical manifestation of sectarian divisions during the 1970s and 1980s. But it is true to say, that, over the generations, Belfast people, particularly working-class people, were born with a radar that made them aware of where they were in the city.

Lacking such instinct could spell danger in the nightlife of Belfast, and most certainly led to many a harsh word and 'scrap' (or street fight). Eventually the political divisions of the city, crackling like an electric storm, were earthed in these intensely intimate and cross-grained inner lives of the city's myriad neighbourhoods. In the late 1960s and early 1970s, what had once been a 'mixed' neighbourhood, where Protestant and Catholic families had 'got on well', experienced the shock of having to face the truth about Belfast's sectarian divisions. Similarly, the traditional Protestant and Catholic areas, which had previously been negotiable by bus or foot when leaving a girl home after a dance, or meeting a pal, or going to a party, became increasingly dangerous and represented a perilous risk upon which few would chance their lives. By the mid-1970s, when assassination squads roamed what became known as 'twilight zones', or interfaces between the dominant working-class districts, Belfast had ceased to be a living city and became, for a decade and more, a ghost town.

Districts played, and still play, a key role in defining the identity of Belfast. Even though there have been extraordinary population shifts within the city over the last twenty-five years, because of intimidation and violence on the one hand, and redevelopment on the other, the sense of being *from* a particular area is strong and lasting. It is a common in many industrial cities.

Put at its simplest, Belfast's history is physically indistinguishable from the industries that were established in the nineteenth and twentieth centuries: linen mills, rope works, tobacco factories, shipbuilding and engineering works.

Erected within this formidable industrial landscape were the streets and houses of the workers. It is not possible to think about Belfast as distinct from this industrial past. Consequently, Belfast is unique in Ireland and has much more in common with Liverpool or Glasgow since the pattern of its streets, as much as the commercial nature of the city, centred on the industrial heartland and little else. Each district had its own factories, its own customs linked to the work practices of the factory, its own destiny and well-being, tied irrevocably to that factory. The Falls, a predominantly Catholic road, had its mills; York Street, in the Protestant lower north side, had the famous Gallaher's tobacco factory; while the shipyards dominated the east of the city. It was a pattern replicated throughout the city, layer by layer, from the dockland up to the prosperous higher roads that circle the outer city, heading for the nearby countryside.

This pattern rapidly disappeared in the post-industrial 1990s. By the early years of the new millennium, developments along the Lagan waterfront transformed parts of the city into apartment villages and multinational 'nowheres', and the birthplace of the

Titanic and other world-renowned passenger liners has been reimagined as the (hugely popular) Titanic Quarter.

Going back forty years, it was a fact of life that those who grew up in the districts surrounding or hugging the industrial shore would become part of it.

The stories of their lives were the stories of the industries in which they worked. Indeed, one reason for the fierceness of the sectarian passion, which has characterised Belfast throughout its history, is the struggle to maintain some standard of living in a city whose economy was (and, of course, remains) fundamentally susceptible to the unpredictable diktats of the government in Westminster.

What was known were the streets where one lived; at least *they* were predictable. Families stayed, generation after generation, and while the men in the house (and sometimes the daughters) might follow work 'across the water' (to Britain) or emigrate farther afield to Canada or Australia, the home territory was a proven ground. Here the rituals of Belfast life were handed down through the calendar of quasi-religious rites and political commemorations.

For the Protestant community, in the main identifying themselves with the union with Britain, their sense that their cultural and political aspirations were different to those of the Irish Catholic community was celebrated through Orange parades and marches. Taking place annually throughout the summer months of July and August, these parades in Belfast were dramatised statements of territorial imperatives and cultural bonding. If Cork or Limerick once had Corpus

Christi, Belfast, which called itself unionist, had 'The Twelfth'.

The serried ranks of bedecked men, in good suits and bowler hats, with sashes and silver insignia pinned onto armlets and lapels, wearing immaculate white gloves and carrying huge silken banners that swayed like canopies in the wind, were an amazing and disturbing sight. Carrying the symbols of the British Crown and imperial past as if they were religious relics, these men assembled in the back streets to demonstrate their loyalty to Queen and Faith and Country.

The major roads and avenues into the centre of the town and beyond the city to a field of worship were transformed on this bizarre occasion and the mood was caught somewhere between that of Mardi Gras and the formal opening of a guild hall. Meanwhile, during this contradictory carnival – which included the pagan-like burning of bonfires on the Eleventh Night, the night before the marching took place, and the sombre declaration of Protestant religious beliefs – the Catholic community either left the city if they could afford to, kept indoors, or observed from a safe distance these men and their followers as they sang and danced through large parts of the city.

Again, much has changed over the years (the Twelfth being rebranded as an 'Orange Fest' comes to mind), and the power of the Twelfth marches of the Orange Order has dwindled into an exotic and effectively symbolic reminder of the divisions that have underscored the city's history and its contested territories, street by street.

From such locations, however, the co-ordinates of life in Belfast were set. What remains on some of these interfaces is the jarring legacy of past conflict and the battle over perceived entitlements and rights.

Antennae of curiosity could identify invisible barriers marking out the social parameters within which people lived. To know where someone lived was tantamount to knowing his or her religion. Received wisdom could then take over.

Moving out from where the City Hall sits inside Donegall Square, the roads and avenues form a compass of religious and cultural division. Rising up out of Donegall Place, Royal Avenue and York Street are the famous districts of the Falls, Shankill and Crumlin – now known as West Belfast.

Turning east towards the Lagan and crossing the river 'over the bridge' are the Newtownards, Albertbridge, Beersbridge and Woodstock districts. The land is densely housed, each neighbourhood a protectorate all on its own.

The predominantly Protestant east side of the city is like a triangular wedge, bordered by one of the longest roads in the city – the Newtownards Road – and by the Castlereagh and Knock roads. Within the triangle are the neighbourhoods of Ballymacarrett, Bloomfield, Strandtown, Ballyhackamore, Castlereagh, Cregagh and Orangefield.

The streetscapes are familiar to anyone who has lived in a provincial, industrial city. East Belfast in particular was defined by that industrial past since shipbuilding physically dominated the horizon. In a literal and imaginative sense, the gantries, sirens, workers' houses and buses, the very sounds and sights of post-war Belfast, were determined by the ups and downs of the shipbuilding orders at the two great industrial sites of Harland and Wolff and Workman and Clark. It may be difficult to appreciate today the extent to which Belfast had once been a leading industrial presence on the international stage. At least three of its industries – shipbuilding, rope works and linen – were the largest of their kind at one time or another. Queen's Island, the symbolic heartland of east Belfast, was the site of the leading shipbuilding business in the world of the 1950s. Terence Brown, the cultural historian and literary critic, has accurately defined the parameters of this industrial world in 'Let's Go To Graceland':

> On any working morning men poured over the bridge that spanned the Lagan and out of the narrow streets of red brick kitchen houses into the shipyard that still saw itself with the Clyde [Glasgow] as a world power in that heroic industry. The rope works were the largest in the world and you could believe it watching the shawlies [women factory workers] teeming around its gates as the hooter sounded summoning them to work through the foggy murk of a part of the city that seemed always in semi-darkness. And there was the aircraft factory and aerodrome too.

Shipbuilding, rope works, aircraft, linen mills, manufacturing of one kind or another; the allied business of commercial and corporation administration; central and local government; service industries – all had turned Belfast into a thriving, industrial, post-war city. Precious wonder then that from John Keats' description in 1818 of 'passing into Belfast through a most wretched suburb' and hearing 'that most disgusting of all noises ... the sound of the [linen mill's] shuttle' to Louis MacNeice's poem 'Valediction', the image of Belfast was exclusively one of a city *defined* by work. MacNeice's Belfast of the 1930s is 'devout and profane and hard':

> Built on reclaimed mud, hammers playing
> in the shipyard,
> Time punched with holes like a steel sheet,
> time
> Hardening the faces, veneering with a grey
> and speckled rime
> The faces under the shawls and caps:
> This was my mother-city, these my paps.

MacNeice was to change his mind and discover beneath the seemingly unchangeable 'outer ugliness and dourness' a deeper reality on his regular visits back to the city during the 1940s and 1950s. But the simple truth of the matter is that east Belfast developed out of the cauldron of heavy industry of modern Belfast. Such a historical reality cannot tell the whole story, however. Around the (now defunct) rope and engineering works, streets of parlour and kitchen houses ('two-ups, two-downs') give way to wider roads and avenues, wealthy parks and gardens, before becoming the countryside. The significance of these distinctions should not be lost to us. Belfast clearly was, and still is, a civic landscape of class distinction. Streetscapes altered, widened and opened out the farther one moved up and away from the city basin and its immediate hinterland. From a very early age, Belfast children learned their place in this scheme of things; it was part of their physical surroundings; assimilating architectural and civic barriers of class as much as absorbing, and sometimes rejecting or transcending as best they could the discreet signs of religious – and hence political–identity.

Accents, too, played a specific, instructive role in deciding within seconds a person's background. For working-class kids who lived in what would approximate today as 'the inner city', the 'posh areas' were merely a step away, in one sense, and in another, a whole world away. To know one's own place was both a source of strength and an inhibition. It was often out on weekend walks through these avenues and parks that one saw the different styles of life counterpoised quite starkly with one's own: houses like mansions; tree-lined driveways; gardens like parks. Sedate, discreet, private. A landscape of imaginative thresholds amounted to a metaphor of the imagination itself. Yet within the intimate, even claustrophobic, closeness of the working-class districts, there were the random open spaces of builders' yards, fugitive rivers and streams, old warehouses, industrial networks and vast walls.

And echoes, if one but knew, of the city's Gaelic palimpsest, charted with such care by Patrick McKay in his *Belfast Place-names and the Irish Language*.

For a young boy or girl who was part of 'a gang of mates', life growing up in such a district was a pendulum-swing between adventure and boredom, dreaming and routine, desire that went against the force of custom, expectation and convention.

Things were close at hand: local cinemas and shops, schools and churches, sport and clubs, bars and walks – all were available within the community. The outside world, whether that be London or some American city, lived in the imagination, fed by film, or the radio, or magazines, or letters and parcels from an aunt or uncle, one of the displaced family members. After the ravages of the Second World War, Belfast, like so many other cities that had experienced the reality of war (the Blitz of 1941 had left over 900 dead and whole areas of the city destroyed), was busy trying to come to terms with peace. But the city had been exposed, in a storm of outrage, blame and shame, to the fact that many of its citizens had been living in appalling housing conditions. Furthermore, the Blitz, having forced tens of thousands from the city, presented startling evidence of the evacuees' poor state of health. The late 1940s and 1950s marked a time when practical solutions to some of these problems were attempted, particularly in the cases of housing, health and education. What did not change, however, were the basic religious and political demographic fault-lines of the city. Some voices predicted trouble if these deep-seated and by now visible grievances of the ordinary people were not addressed. As Jonathan Bardon remarked, while 'the Second World War had been far more harrowing that the First' for the citizens of Belfast, 'the sense of optimism and hope seemed stronger than in 1918; to a large extent this was justified'.

THREE

Born in 1945 in east Belfast, as the Second World War ended and optimism and hope grew, Van Morrison's early years followed a traditional pattern, at least on the surface. His surname in Ulster draws together the province's Gaelic roots. According to Robert Bell, Morrison is among 'the thirty most numerous names in Scotland' while its Irish origin Ó Muirgheasáin (from *Muirgheas*, meaning 'sea valour') comes from County Donegal, the most westerly of the Ulster counties. Indeed the exchange and cross-fertilisation between Ulster and Scotland are embedded in the Morrison name itself.

Other references to Morrison pick out the historical and cultural connections between Ulster and Scotland and the mythopoetical connections with Scandinavia; while running consistently through such sources there is the recurring elements of music and poetry. No matter how one views the veracity of family trees, the unmistakably Irish and Scottish cultural and social meshing of Morrison's own surname provides a myth of origin which Morrison would explore in his music. Precious wonder too that his famous 1973/74 band and production company, Caledonia, should take its name from the Latin for northern Britain, and refers to a native of ancient Scotland. The cultural voyage that Morrison undertook in the early 1970s was in effect a journey back in time to such mythical beginnings.

At the age of five, Van Morrison went to Elm Grove Primary School, a stone's throw away from his home at 125 Hyndford Street, just off the Beersbridge Road. The school led on to Lady Dixon's playing fields; across the road lay a clutch of streets with such pastoral names as Avoneil and Flora, and the historically laden Mayflower, while the Conn's Water ran through the district, serving as a reminder of an earlier time in the late sixteenth and seventeenth centuries when it gave its name to a small coastal port of some importance.

Ballymacarret, the townland, takes its name from the Gaelic, and means town of 'Mac Art'. It is a staunchly Protestant and loyalist area. Orange halls, band halls, working men's clubs and bars and, more recently, leisure and day centres, nursery schools and shopping malls front the redeveloped housing estates that sit alongside the numerous places of worship: Church of Ireland, Presbyterian, Methodist, Baptist, Non-Conformist and several evangelical sects, such as Jehovah's Witnesses and Elim Pentecostal. Morrison, like most of his contemporaries, went briefly to Sunday school and attended church. In the grand St Donard's Church of Ireland at the Bloomfield intersection, barely ten minutes' walk from the leafy Cyprus Avenue and suburban North Road, the setting for some of his great early lyrics, Morrison would have heard an austere lesson in Christian faith, duty and reserve, whereas in the evangelical meetings, an energetic and Americanised version of the gospel would speak of a spirited mission of redemption, the Blood of the Lamb and joy in Christ.

Protestantism was everywhere. From the Union Jack flying above the Orange halls to billboards proclaiming proverbial wisdom from the Bible to assemblies and religious instruction at school, it was impossible not to absorb the teaching and cultural values of the Protestant Church. In working-class east Belfast, as in other working-class areas throughout the city, Protestantism was a very wide Church indeed, embracing mainstream traditions such as Anglicanism, Presbyterianism and Methodism, as well as the distinctively evangelical.

Protestants often took an *à la carte* attitude to their worship. While membership of a particular church passed down through families, generation by generation, it was not uncommon for mothers in particular to shop around and send their children to different churches under the broad umbrella of Protestantism.

There was the 'respectable' Church of Ireland, for the upwardly mobile who sought a place alongside the satisfied burghers of the district; the down-to-earth Presbyterians, who tended also towards the political; the somewhat introverted Methodists and a panoply of different sects and breakaway groups, who asked for a much more personal commitment from their flock. 'There is in Ulster,' remarks Steve Bruce, 'a pietistic evangelical tradition which sees religion as an alternative to the ways of the world and which stresses the importance of avoiding worldly contamination. Especially strong in working-class areas, a gospel hall and Pentecostal tradition serves as a way out of the everyday world.'

The atmosphere of such gospel halls and evangelical meeting houses could not be more different from either the high-bred Church of Ireland or the Presbyterian Scottish Gothic. Built on wastelands, in derelict sites of one kind or another, at corners and in out-of-the-way places, the huts of the evangelical revivalist preachers attracted a small but steady flow of the curious and disenchanted. Over the years, such sects developed and grew and, with them, the faithful paid for and built grand tabernacles in which fully flown Crusades (religious ceremonies) took place, along with open-air rallies.

It is interesting to note that the best-known evangelical preacher to come from Northern Ireland, the Reverend Ian Paisley, preached an invitation sermon on Christmas Day 1945 at the Ravenhill Evangelical Mission Church in working-class east Belfast before becoming the pastor at that church. Within his lifetime he was to create a new sect, the Free Presbyterian Church, one of whose imposing buildings straddles the Ravenhill Road and receives busloads of worshippers every week.

That said, the sects are, and always have been, a minority in Belfast. Among the working class, such sects are often seen as obsessive, dour and self-righteous. Their influence fades into the wider Calvinist atmosphere that pervaded the city throughout the post-war period and well into the 1960s. There was a governing ethos of Sabbatarian rule, when all forms of entertainment were frowned upon on a Sunday – public bars, clubs, parks, cinemas and (most) dance halls were closed; television was not allowed; blinds were often pulled or curtains closed, and it was considered improper to play on the streets. The lasting negative effects of such a puritanical society upon those who grew up in it are obviously profound and mark to the very core the individual sensibility. There is, however, another side to this story. For the dominant religious force of Protestantism also carried, in different forms, a contradictory sense of poetic language, as well as choral and lyrical music.

While the routines of an evangelical meeting might appear to be soulless in comparison with, say, the ceremony of Catholic mass or the pomp of High Church, the language of 'being healed' and 'saved', the plain witness of one man's voice bearing testimony to finding the Lord, has a poignancy and theatricality all its own. Textually based upon the Old Testament, adamant in its fundamentalist convictions of right and wrong, sin and forgiveness, speaking out against self-deception and seeking the Lord through being born again, the language and performance of such preachers provided as much entertainment as it did spiritual guidance. The minister, or pastor or preacher brings his religion to the congregation so that they might see the light and error of their ways and gain thereby a new sense of security about who and what they are, having found themselves through salvation.

The evangelical power of conversion and redemption is drenched in the imagery of a simpler life, spurning illusions and the allure of false gods. It is a forceful, dogmatic and profoundly individualistic faith that earnestly wrestles with issues of 'truth' and the pursuit of the transcendental in everyday, working life.

Hardly surprising then that the district in which Morrison grew up should include a Calvin Street. Protestantism was, after all, not solely 'a religion' but a way of life. As Morrison's ironic understatement has it, 'We didn't go to church all the time, but it was a very churchy atmosphere in the sense that that's the way it is in Northern Ireland.'

If Protestantism was like the air one breathed, the ground one walked on was assumed to be British. Post-war Belfast was an emphatically British city. Belfast had a recent history similar to other British cities, from the war effort to the Blitz and the thousands of American GIs, to the victory parades and ration books; the city itself was also marked with bomb sites and pre-fabricated houses.

There were the local connections with Scotland – geographical as much as industrial – and the political-economic associations and cultural identifications between a majority of the Protestant community and the mainland, and a not insubstantial proportion of the Catholic community as well.

Leaving for work in Scotland and England (less so in Wales) was part of the Belfast way of life. There was the historical exchange within the British Isles as job opportunities fell in Ulster and rose elsewhere. Men would travel and settle, sometimes taking their families with them, sometimes not. This 'internal' emigration, with family members eventually establishing homes away from Belfast – in Glasgow, London, Leeds, Birmingham, Newcastle, Liverpool – was a fairly common practice from quite early on in the twentieth century.

In my own family, for instance, one grandfather emigrated to Canada and worked for many years there before moving to Nottingham; his wife's sister left Belfast in the 1920s and settled in London, only to return once every ten years, and her daughter left London in the 1960s and lived and worked in Belfast for some time before returning to London. Such journeying back and forth has followed personal needs and at the same time reflected wider economic and cultural pressures over the past century. This 'emigration' accelerated at various critical moments, such as the Depression of the late 1920s and mid-to-late 1930s, with emigration farther afield to Canada, America and Australia. The early 1970s and through the years of the Troubles had also seen an exodus, particularly among the young.

It was not always thus, however. Workers could also travel *into* Northern Ireland, although it was a protected labour market, given the scandalously high unemployment figures in the province. Permits were required for anyone born outside to work inside. Be that as it may, there was a constant flow of workers across the Irish Sea. I recall, at a Christmas party in suburban north London in 1986, meeting the Scottish father of the very English hostess. He was in his eighties and had worked, he told me with ironic pride, on the building of Stormont, the Northern Ireland parliament buildings that were opened in 1932 by the then Prince of Wales, later Edward VIII.

The imposing neo-classical house of colonial parliament, visible from all over Belfast, dominates an impressively landscaped site on the Upper Newtownards Road in the east of the city. The old worker told me that there were many Scottish craftsmen who worked on the building, having been brought in especially from Glasgow, including gold leaf specialists whose artwork, originally used for the grand interiors of ocean liners, can still be seen on the ceilings and cornices of this once all-powerful seat of central power.

Stormont's extended political heyday was between 1932 and 1972 when the British prime minister, Edward Heath, suspended the Stormont government as a result of the rapidly deteriorating political situation in Northern Ireland. The building came to symbolise the ignominious failure of the provincial parliament. Its fifty years of institutional life since the partition of Ireland in 1922 had not addressed the religious and cultural divisions that were so potently marked in the North. While the economic basis of the state was deeply indebted to British investment, the government in Westminster also underwrote its educational and social welfare system.

For barely twenty years or so, in the post Second World War, pre-Troubles period (roughly between the late 1940s and late 1960s), the provincial government had within its grasp the opportunity to redress the sense of injustice and discrimination many Catholics experienced throughout Northern Ireland, which was in no place more keenly felt than in Belfast. That failure of political will was undeniably the key turning point. It acted as a catalyst for the sectarian warfare, political jingoism and paramilitary power struggles that would eventually claim the lives of over 3,000 people and maim, physically and emotionally, hundreds of thousands of lives in the North, the Republic, in Britain and elsewhere.

However, most historians agree that the slow signs of prosperity that started to show in the local post-war Northern economy, with the combined shipyards employing 20,000 workers in 1959, and the steps taken to better the living standards of ordinary people, were all linked, in the public mind at least, with the continued union of Northern Ireland with Britain. School books, radio programmes and regional television, when it eventually came (May 1955), accepted and underscored the status quo. There was an unquestionable belief that Belfast had weathered the storm and that it could look forward, in some manner, to an improved future, certainly if measured by pre-war standards.

A new health system was established and in 1947 the Education Act allowed for, amongst other items, free, public, secondary-intermediate education. This catered for all children from five to fifteen years of age. The grammar-school sector expanded and further education centres opened to cope with the rising lower-middle-class aspirations. To a young boy, moving between home, school and just knocking around, such concerns were irrelevant, and the main preoccupation of Van Morrison's childhood years was music. This would not have been uncommon.

Throughout working-class Belfast, different forms of music proliferated, particularly the playing of instruments. Often associated with ceremonial occasions, a tradition exists of flute bands, silver bands and military bands, which filled the air not only during the marching seasons of July through to August but throughout the year as well, with band practice an accepted and regular meeting place. This tradition is extensive and has been subject to very little research and much misunderstanding.

The Orange Party tunes – like the rebel songs of the Nationalist tradition – form only one part, and a greatly fluctuating part, in the tradition as a whole. The tunes of these different kinds of bands vary greatly, from hymns to ballads to popular 'classics' (title tracks from television programmes, for example) to marching tunes. The principle of selection has generally been what is popular at any given time, along with the ceremonial music drawn from the British military tradition: from 'Rock of Ages' to 'Z Cars' to a Beatles number to 'The Dam Busters' to a sentimental Percy French melody for good measure.

As the Rev. Gary Hastings, an authority on Northern musical traditions, explained to me, the great desire of late-nineteenth and twentieth-century Northern Protestant marching music was for respectability: a demonstration of community discipline and self-regard, modelled along military lines.

Having moved from the infantryman's fife and drum to the civilian flute, snare drum, Scottish pipes, accordion (and very rarely, the powerful Lambeg drum), the band music provided a cultural backdrop to life in Northern Ireland. Its message was double-edged: on the one hand, it was music to be played for its own sake and heartily enjoyed. On the other hand, it was 'Protestant' music insofar as it maintained, on particular public and state occasions, cultural distinctions between that community and its fellow Catholic Northerners. It was music played on the streets and in the parks; broadcast on the radio and featured in church. Indeed, as the Rev. Hastings pointed out, the role of the church in maintaining public interest in ceremonial music is central. In one Protestant church after another, religion and entertainment met.

Furthermore, through the socialising role of its own organisations, such as the Boys' and Girls' Brigades, the Scouting Movement and so forth, the language, imagery and morality of Bible, Faith and Empire meshed into one common fabric. The church, in other words, was a social place, and music played a crucial role in unifying the community.

Again there are differences within the broad Protestant faith. As the Rev. Hastings described it, the upbeat clapping and religious 'come-all-ye's of the evangelical fundamentalist sects that grew out of Ulster contrasted sharply with the Church of Ireland and its organ-based, choral hymns and remote, thoughtful rituals. At a much more practical level, of course, with so many bandsmen and bandswomen in the community as a whole – for the Catholic community responded with its own orders, religious and cultural societies, and their own bands and days of celebration – the pool of musicians with basic playing skills and knowledge of music was extensive, given the population of Belfast and the province at large.

This dominant civic music, powerful and popular as it has been throughout the brief history of the Northern Ireland state, could not totally eclipse 'the tiny musical survivals' (the phrase is the Rev. Hasting's) of an older tradition, a folk music.

This technically astute and intensive music, played on the fiddle, flute, melodeon, uilleann pipes and bodhrán, was basically dancing music. When sung, it usually retold sad stories of lost love and emigration or praise for a beloved local place.

It is an exciting music driven by powerful but simple repetitive rhymes. Unlike the mass involvement, relatively speaking, of marching bands, the individual fiddler, flute player or piper addresses a closed audience of fellow musicians, listeners or a set of dancers. Even the formal concert setting seems unnatural.

The roots of the music are rural, and before the advent of radio or television, traditional music was the form of musical entertainment. But with the explosion of musical options that came in the wake of the Second World War and the much wider availability of radio, cinema and eventually television, the tradition went underground. Individual musicians scattered, often in search of work in cities elsewhere in Ireland, Britain and North America. Like blues guitarists and musicians, if they travelled away from home they either fell silent or kept within their own ethnic communities. Audiences at home shrank as the new forms of orchestrated popular music took over in the late 1940s and 1950s.

Ciarán Mac Mathúna, a leading collector of Irish folk music, reminds us of a time when in Ireland 'middle-class people laughed at this kind of [traditional] music, when it was considered just good enough for the countryside, and when city people and the middle class didn't like or didn't want to know about this music'. Back in the 1950s and 1960s, Mac Mathúna recalls, 'on a long dance late in the night [the band] might have thrown in an Irish dance for a bit of a laugh, but that was all'.

Belfast was different in that, during the early 1960s, as the twenty-four-year-old Morrison described it in an interview published in *Rolling Stone* in July 1970, there was an important, if limited, crossover taking place in the city:

> Memphis Slim has been in Belfast; Jesse Fuller, Champion Jack Dupree, John Lee Hooker's been there. They've got folk clubs and rock clubs there, but it's got

nothing to do with the English scene. In fact, I'd go so far as to say it doesn't have much to do with [the] Irish scene either, it's just Belfast. It's got its own identity, it's got its own people ... it's just a different race, a different breed of people. There's a lot of changes there, too. Like the McPeakes on one hand, and some others of us on the other hand, and they're open to all kinds of music, not just one thing. Maybe a third of the people that are into R & B would go to hear the McPeakes.

Morrison has also referred in other interviews to his having started off 'in folk music', which can be taken as shorthand for the musician as an individual who first learns this genre and then puts his or her individual stamp on what has gone before. A further interesting note from the 1970 interview is Morrison's views on blues and traditional Irish music as essentially linked in the context of Belfast of the previous decade. The imaginative shift from Irish traditional music to blues and jazz, which seemed quite natural in Morrison's recollection of the late 1950s and early 1960s, had begun to show political strains by the early 1970s. While I was travelling around the city and becoming more interested in traditional music, I became aware of a 'ghettoisation' of the music, despite the best efforts of many of the musicians and a substantial part of the audience as well. Morrison's good fortune allowed him to encounter traditional Irish music without the political-cultural freight it was expected to bear during the next twenty years and more. More importantly though, there was the very early exposure to what Morrison has continuously acknowledged as the key influence of his early years in Belfast: his father. 'There was probably only ten big collectors [of blues and jazz] in Belfast and [my father] was one of them.' Alongside these recordings played to the young Morrison, he has spoken about his mother's love of singing songs such as 'I'll Take You Home Again, Kathleen', 'Sweet Sixteen' and 'Goodnight Irene', as well as the popular ballads of the day.

It was coincidental, of course, that during the 1950s Britain was experiencing a skiffle (acoustic folk-jazz) and trad jazz revival, inspired in part by the blues played by black American artists. Morrison has often cited his days playing 'in a skiffle group' and his having 'started off in folk music'. The historical picture has been drawn in great detail and imaginative sympathy by musicologists such as Charlie Gillett in *The Sound of the City*, Lawrence Cohn in *Nothing but the Blues* and by participants like George Melly in *Revolt into Style*.

Belfast was no exception, and many of the leading lights of the trad jazz revival played concerts in Belfast during the mid-to-late 1950s. Witness, for example, the English poet Philip Larkin, who lived in Belfast and worked as a librarian at Queen's University, as he recalls in the introduction to his record diary *All What Jazz* the following scene in the Plaza Ballroom, Chichester Street, Belfast in 1954: 'A thousand people squashed into the smallish Plaza dance hall and a thousand more milled outside, the more enterprising getting in through a small square window in the men's lavatory ... Lonnie Donegan would come forward with his impersonation of Lead Belly.'

Nine-year-old Morrison was back home in Hyndford Street listening to the original records of Lead Belly, an artist whom Morrison would much later identify as one of the strongest earliest influences on him, along with other great blues players such as Muddy Waters, Sonny Terry and Brownie Mc Ghee.

George Melly's point in *Revolt into Style* (the title comes from Thom Gunn's poem on Elvis Presley) is well worth bearing in mind too. He wrote about the violent world of which Lead Belly sang: 'Lead Belly was in prison twice on murder charges and had a near psychopathic personality. Donegan's version was safely distanced from that world. Its violence and harshness was make-believe and in retrospect he sounds more like George Formby than Huddie Ledbetter.'

The connection made at such an early age might also account for the emphasis, which Morrison had alluded to in interviews, of the emotional bonds and cultural aspirations many Belfast people shared with North America as much as with Britain.

In the early 1950s, Morrison's father visited America, worked there for a time and considered bringing out his wife and son. It was also during this period that Morrison has said he became hooked on the radio, listening to *Voice of America*, and clearly the young Morrison's exposure to real blues at such an early age had a profound and lasting effect.

It is important to recall, too, the afterglow in Belfast of the 1950s left by the many thousands of American troops, including black GIs, who had been stationed throughout the North prior to D-Day. Having brought with them not only bubblegum and cigarettes, but also their own styles of music and dance, they took over the floor of ballrooms such as the Plaza (built in 1942) with an uncharacteristic flamboyance and glamour.

Undoubtedly, the Belfast that Morrison knew growing up was split-levelled. There was the orthodox, self-satisfied official exterior, as formidable as the City Hall itself, expecting its citizens to believe that all was well and that things could only get better, particularly for the city's loyal sons and daughters.

On the other hand, there were, throughout the city, men and women such as George and Violet Morrison, and their son, Ivan, whose primary interest was music. It was an alternative world that permeated the pieties and structure of the known and accepted society experiencing, as it then was in the mid-1950s, something of an upswing and expansion, including the widening provision of educational opportunities.

One of the new schools established around this time, in 1957, and officially opened the following year (3 May 1958), was Orangefield Boys' School. A little later, Orangefield Girls' School was established on the same site and Grosvenor Grammar School, on an adjacent site, with the result that there were then three schools catering for the burgeoning second-level educational needs of the neighbourhood.

Orangefield's headmaster was a dynamic yet cool-tempered Cambridge-educated scholar called John Malone. He was a liberal who had fought against the staid and complacent educational authorities in Belfast. He sought to provide in Orangefield a genuinely comprehensive education for the working-class children of east Belfast. The school curriculum, however, was to include not only the standard grounding in applied trades and clerkly professions which most, if not all, of its students would eventually join; it also set out to encourage a wider – some would say, experimental – learning in music, theatre, politics, and, of course, sport.

The school's young and more experienced teachers alike supported Malone's vision. His beliefs were, however, to be severely tested, given the deep-seated cultural prejudices of the 1950s and early 1960s. Work was considered to be the logical and sole reason for the education of ordinary working-class boys and girls. This was in keeping with the dominant religious and political ethos of Protestant unionism of the time. Orangefield conceded, indeed actively endorsed, these principles in naming the four school 'houses' – or fraternities – after local engineering works, such as Sirocco and Bryson.

However, as the school established itself, it achieved an academic recognition beyond the original remit and throughout the 1960s was identified as Belfast's leading progressive 'comprehensive' school, with pupils of quite diverse backgrounds attending from all over the city, alongside those drawn from the

45

immediate catchment area of east Belfast. We catch a glimpse of this frission when Morrison describes his years at Orangefield (1956–60):

> There was no school for people like me. I mean, we were freaks in the full sense of the word because either we didn't have the bread to go to the sort of school where we could sit down and do our thing, or that type of school didn't exist. Most of what was fed me really didn't help me that much later.

Things were to change at that very school in a matter of years, but Morrison had moved on by then. However, given the conservatism, snobbery and civic priorities of Belfast in the mid-to-late 1950s, it is hardly surprising that Morrison, along with others of his age, should have looked for something else. Blues music became that voice of dissent, but it was fundamentally an emotional reaction, not a political act. Black musicians like Lead Belly, Jelly Roll Morton and jazz figures like Charlie Parker embodied a way of life and represented a kind of lifestyle with which the young Morrison could identify.

FOUR

From an early age, Morrison had picked up a guitar bought for him by his father. Armed with his guitar, he obviously found himself, like so many others of that time and since, with his own fate literally in his hands. Within no time, he was playing and imitating the records he had been listening to and was looking for the chance to perform. The crucial difference with Morrison, as the years between the late 1950s and 1967 show, is that he was not only discovering a powerfully focused talent; he was also encountering the world through his music and the subculture of this world, which was to be an all-embracing focus. If playing music was just a job, as he had repeatedly said, it was some job. 'The original idea in the British Isles was just to get out of your working-class environment and make a living out of playing music. It's that simple. I just wanted to be a musician, full-time. That was the ultimate goal.'

Precious wonder that in his later work of the 1980s and 1990s, Morrison would seek to rediscover imaginatively through his music that early home where it had all started. The mature Morrison's realisation is chastened, however, by the fact that it was his very talent that had cast him out in the first place. Morrison's lyrics are driven by that sense of contradiction: the intimacy and quietude of home is shaken by doubt and uncertainty about its ability to sustain the demands of the artistic and professional world beyond. Morrison's work as a musician and singer-songwriter negotiates this tension, whether in the intensely lyrical passages of *Astral Weeks* (1967), the rage of 'Listen to the Lion' (1974) or work of the 1990s, from *Hymns to the Silence* (1991) to the present.

Morrison took the traditional east-Belfast route, and was apprenticed to one of the local engineering works. When this proved unsatisfactory, Morrison worked in a meat-cleaning factory, in a chemist's shop, and then went freelance, cleaning windows around the Orangefield area. Each job was secondary to the real business of playing with the ever-changing line-up of local bands, from Deanie Sands and the Javelins, later The Thunderbolts, to their formation in 1960 of The Monarchs. His professional career can be said to have started with his early gigs with The Monarchs, when he played the saxophone.

The popular musical background throughout Ireland, north and south, at this time featured the dance-hall showbands, ceilidh music and pub-based folk, modelled on and derived from groups like the Clancy Brothers. The showband scene was an ersatz mixture of cover versions of 'pop' hits from America and Britain. Whatever about his private education in blues and jazz, Morrison had to work his way through the reality of audience expectations at the time. The trad jazz revival in the 1950s had more or less petered out and returned to minority status, along with Irish traditional music and folk singing.

There was, however, an additional influence at play. Morrison was starting to make connections through his reading with the work of the Beat Generation, in particular the iconic autobiographical novel *On the Road* (1957), written by Jack Kerouac. Kerouac's fiction, such as *On the Road* and *The Dharma Bums* (1958), represents paths to freedom through the group of fugitives who spurn the white, puritanical, work-obsessed post-war America of their own time in favour of a life of self-obsessed experiment and an indeterminate future on the West Coast. Kerouac also wrote aggressively in his own voice, a style of conversational address, buoyed up with jazz-talk and immediate access to poetic vision:

> It was a wonderful night. Central City is two miles high; at first you get drunk on the altitude, then you get tired, and there's a fever in your soul. We approached the lights around the opera house down the narrow dark street; then we took a sharp right and hit some old saloons with swinging doors. Most of the tourists were in the opera. We started off with a few extra-size beers. There was a player piano. Beyond the back door was a view of

> mountainsides in the moonlight. I let out
> a yahoo. The night was on.

For the intense teenager hanging out in Belfast, these words must have sounded like a new gospel. As fellow Monarchs member George Jones remarked, Morrison 'wrote poetry. It was deep ... most of us didn't know what he was talking about'. Kerouac's reverence for jazz, too, would not have gone amiss, as black blues artists and the mention of poetic figures such as Rimbaud must have inspired Morrison in the same way as it had influenced Bob Dylan and The Doors singer, Jim Morrison.

It is, of course, all too easy, with hindsight, to see that in those first few years of the 1960s, Morrison was gaining the professional experience needed to maintain a 'career' as a musician. More importantly, he was forming the attitude and the belief that such a life was actually possible. There can be no inevitability about such desires, as if Morrison planned his career step by step. Far from it. He moved where and when he could and took what chances came his way, something he has been quite clear about himself:

> Picture the situation. Put yourself working
> in showbands, touring in buses with seven
> or eight people, sleeping in parks, having
> no money. Put yourself through working
> the clubs in Germany, on up to when the
> r'n'b movement thing was happening in
> the 60s; put yourself through being in a

situation where you're supposed to be a somebody. The thing that has carried me through this is the time I put in when I was nobody. When I was with Them, it was anti-climatic. All right so I'm a star but I don't want it. I just do my music.

In an effort to secure more gigs, the five-man Monarchs added four musicians to their original line-up and became a showband. This meant that while they were no longer 'a group', they could now play in the bigger Belfast ballrooms. The four-piece band (drums, bass, lead guitar and singer) was supplemented with keyboards and brass instruments.

One of the new additions, Ronnie Osborne, had joined from a brass band. The Monarchs were, in effect, caught between two worlds, and the next year and more tells their own story of musical aspirations confronting show-business reality. The ballroom requirements were simple: play the music that the audience was hearing on the radio and buying records of in the shops. The people were there to dance; the band was there to entertain. After all, dancing was a night out.

The ballrooms themselves were imitation palaces; the showbands were dressed up in distinctive monogrammed liveries (a crown for The Monarchs) that fell somewhere between quasi-military uniforms (underlined by the somewhat mechanical dance steps on stage) and formal wedding attire. The showbands also provided flashes of showmanship within an ongoing, self-contained and predictable musical set. The music was all about polish, and the majority of the musicians were highly skilled in imitating all sorts of music. Their inner musical inclinations were quite subservient to the wishes of the audience, ballroom owner and promoter. While some 'hotter' numbers could be smuggled in as breathing spaces between dances, or to show off one of the band's players, in the main they replicated 'hits', irrespective of whether they were pop, country 'n' western or 'jokey' ballads:

> May the bird of paradise fly up your nose;
> May an elephant caress you with its toes.

As George Jones told journalist Vincent Power, 'There was no other outlet.' Morrison's own comments underscore the commercial realities of the time: 'You couldn't work properly if you didn't have [a horn section]. All the showbands had horn sections and a lot of them were really good, like the Royal Showband, The Dixielanders, The Swingtime Aces, Clipper Carlton.' So what The Monarchs were doing in 1960, ahead of time, was including in their repertoire, alongside the pop material, some material from the R & B American style of Ray Charles and Muddy Waters. Given the times that were in it, such innovation was a risky business, but frustrating nonetheless for Morrison, who obviously wanted to push further into that terrain.

After a spell away from The Monarchs, Morrison and the by-now seven-piece band decided to try to make it abroad and they travelled to Scotland in 1962.

Behind them were five years or so of playing the dance halls and ballrooms of their own locality – Belfast and the surrounding counties. Now they had left this behind, albeit travelling only as far as Scotland; the harsher realities of being away from home, on the road and looking for work must have pressed in upon the unlikely group of lads.

It is a story that has been told many times since of prospecting, buoyed up with the two Glaswegians whom they had met in Belfast. The Belfast group travelled around Scotland expecting more work than they could actually find, and so they decided to travel south to London.

This is the stuff of myth-making, of course: the provincial encounters with the cosmopolitan culture which was such a defining feature of the 'Swinging Sixties': pop culture, literature, film and theatre. As George Jones recounts, they drove directly to London from Aberdeen: 'We were really tired. We just kept driving to try and find a place to bunk down. We felt dejected. We were ready to go home, but didn't want to give in to our parents.' All were in their teens; The Monarchs were in London in 1962 in a van. All they had was their own personalities and the knowledge and feeling for a different kind of music. It was to sustain the group for a year or so, including a tour of Britain and Germany, before their return to Belfast in 1963. This was a crucial time for Morrison's development – between these years (1962–7), he would experience the commercial exigencies of the music business, but also begin the real struggle for his own artistic independence, an abiding theme of his work ever since.

Morrison records at the very heart of his work a series of dilemmas. He has spoken of these in the interviews he has given throughout a career that spans half a century; interviews that reveal him as a vastly experienced and uncompromising critic of the contemporary world and the fate of genuine artistic endeavour in that world.

As a musician, all Morrison need do is entertain (what he calls 'earning my living'), but there is also a profound desire to communicate 'more' than that; as a performer, there is the conflict between protecting the individual, private self while dealing with, and in, a mass-market music business that thrives on and exploits disclosure. There is also the never-ending struggle for balance as Morrison's music aspires to some form of genuine spiritual experience while simultaneously contending with the rigours, routines and business of touring a band.

Running through these emotionally charged and intently artistic issues, Morrison's writing lights upon the imagery of Protestant mysticism while the songs, reaching for rapture, recollect human limitation and loss against which his voice and lyrics protest.

Morrison's time with Them consisted of a brief period of full-on musical and performative energy on stage. The band, formed in Belfast late in 1963, captured the mood of the city. Indeed, from this period in the early 1960s, Belfast was to produce a number of bands who played a mix of R & B and blues. They lived on stage performances, as Morrison has made clear many times, at such venues as Belfast's Maritime Hotel. As a live band, the energy of their performances was not captured in the singles, such as 'Don't Start Crying Now', 'Baby, Please Don't Go', 'Gloria' (1964), 'Here Comes the Night' (1965) or the albums they released, *Them* (1965) and *Them Again* (1966).

The raw, almost belligerent energy of Morrison's voice spoke directly of and to a generation coming into its own during the early 1960s. But there was much more involved than brash display. In 'The Story of Them', written by Morrison, the narrative recounts a Belfast literally opening out, as:

> Blues come rolling down Royal Avenue
> Won't stop by the City Hall
> Just a few steps away
> You can look up at the Maritime
>   Hotel ...

Morrison's searching elaboration of the syllables of his tale is mocked by the quizzing lead guitar as the emerging generation in the actual story stare back at the world with bristling self-preoccupation. 'The Story of Them' is a mini-epic sung to the laid-back rhythms of talking blues:

> When friends were friends and company
>   was right
> We'd drink and talk and sing all through
>   the night

> And morning came leisurely and bright.
> Down town we'd walk and passers-by
> Would shudder with delight. Hmnn –
> Good times.

The languor of Morrison's voice is underscored by the band's consistently fugitive and disconsolate backing. The characteristic note is of a past that has slipped away: 'It was a gas'. The instant retake on the band's life on the stage of The Maritime tells a rhetorical story about defiance and disdain ('We don't care'), which is dramatised through the inflections of Morrison's Belfast accent. As he plays with individual words and toys with occasional harmonica rushes, Morrison's voice evokes an imaginative terrain that is in the mind's eye, summoned by the names and sounds of places and things:

> Barred from pubs, clubs and dancing halls
> Made the scene at the Spanish Rooms on
>   the Falls
> And then four pints of that scrumpy was
>   enough to have you
> Out of your mind, climbing up the walls,
>   out of your mind.

Acknowledging the help of 'The Three Jays' – Gerry McKenna, Gerry McKervey and Jimmy Conlon who were young promoters on the music scene in the early 1960s – Morrison laments, 'It was something else then.' With a surprising lack of sentimentality or nostalgia, questions are asked and answered in an impersonation of the audience's view of what they (the audience) are looking at on stage. 'The Story of Them' is Morrison in dramatic monologue:

> People say, 'Who are Them?' or 'What are
>   Them?'
> That little one sings and that big one plays
>   the guitar
> With a thimble on his finger, runs it up and
>   down the strings;
> Bass player don't say much:
> I think they are all a little bit touched.

The colloquial idiom of 'a little bit touched' runs alongside the self-consciousness of the whole number and the ambiguous, contradictory relationship between band and audience, time and place is summed up in the simple declaration:

> Wild, sweaty, crude, ugly and mad,
> Sometimes just a little bit sad.
> Yeah, they sneered and all,
> But up there we were just having a ball.
> We are Them, take it or leave it.
> Do you know they took it,
> And they kept coming.

Morrison ends the songs with a farewell: 'Just a little bit sad / gonna walk for a while / wish it well'. This is a gesture that features in so many of his lyrics as the insider leaves the scene with the knowledge that a return is always going to be qualified by the fact of leaving.

What is clear from the recordings of Morrison with Them is the self-belief and confidence in what they are doing on stage. As he says in 'The Story of Them', 'The people kept coming'. In The Maritime and the other small clubs around Belfast, an audience was building up for the peculiar mix of blues, R & B and a folk-jazz reminiscent of Dylan. This growing audience, mainly young, working-class and lower-middle-class, had previously been invisible. They were children of the welfare state, and the first generation to really benefit from the steady if slow upswing in economic fortunes during the late 1950s and the early 1960s.

According to David Harkness, 'Material conditions improved for many in both communities in these years, and many began to move into new housing areas where religions intermingled and good neighbours were found amongst traditional foes.'

Notwithstanding what Harkness also refers to as the 'ingrained unemployment problem' that afflicted the Northern economy, the mid-1960s reflected, at least on the surface, an image of the provincial capital as vibrant and in touch with what was going on in the world.

Variously billed as Belfast's Jazz Club and Rhythm & Blues Club, The Maritime Hotel in College Square North was a merchant seaman's hostel built (on the site of a former Royal Irish Constabulary station) in 1945 by the British Sailors' Society.

Situated with its back ironically shunning two of the city's most famous educational institutes, the Royal

Belfast Academical Institution ('Inst') and the College of Technology, and equidistant from the city centre and the bottom of the Falls Road, the club in 1964 was the focus for Queen's University students and the outward-going and confident working-class young.

In this most work-orientated of cities, where status and prestige was intrinsically linked to one's 'steady' job and prospects, the students had an identity of their own. In meeting with those working-class kids in their late teens or early twenties, a brief crossover took place that was to last during the mid-years of the 1960s. In passing, it's true that with the eruption of the Troubles in the late 1960s and early 1970s, The Maritime, alongside other 'clubs' such as Sammy Houston's in Great Victoria Street, provided a chance for kids of every religion and none to get together. Such thoughts would have been far from the minds of these kids at the time, however; all that mattered was the music. For many working-class kids, seeing students looking like 'beatniks' would have had a greater effect on them than what church they attended.

The experience must have been something of a liberation from the conventions of previous generations when 'going out' meant dressing 'proper'. For the general rule had been that once the dungarees, factory overalls or shop clothes were taken off, it was time to 'dress up'. The men, older brothers, uncles and next-door neighbours had their hair quiffed and immaculately cut, were after-shaved, had the thin bar of white handkerchief in the breast pocket of the

Burton's Italian suit, and the required showing of shirt cuffs with the monogrammed links and gleaming Chelsea boots. Their girls were in dresses and imitation furs or 'swag coats', always carrying in their handbags the silver, dagger-like, back-combing comb to preserve the look. A Friday or Saturday night was the chance to be part of a picture show in which everyone who ventured out had style and became an actor.

Belfast's city centre, with the light spilling out from the plate-glass shop-front windows and the perpetual flow of buses, was actually like a stage set for drama. And drama there was. Lovers met 'downtown', had drinks, and went to the pictures or to a classy ballroom. There could be bloody and at times vicious fist fights or worse for the macho, vain or vanquished in this most intensely proud and symbolic display of male proprieties, which their women would sometimes imitate.

There could be operatic rows between dates in shop doorways or at street corners and on buses. Indeed, to circumnavigate Belfast's city centre on a weekend was often an experience in itself. For it was to watch (but not too intently, for fear of ending up involved!) the clash between the theatrical and the everyday. Working life confronted itself with time off and was exposed in turn to the dream world of entertainment, leisure and possibility. A world, it was commonly believed, which 'the students' perpetually inhabited.

With their 'long' hair, wearing whatever came their way, from duffle coats to old school blazers, flared pants, ex-army leather jackets, polo-necks, jeans, suede shoes and Norfolk jackets, the students defied (if only for a few years) the working ethos of the city. They were an unknown quantity and, in a sense, Queen's students of the time lived in a quarantined world. They had a fool's pardon when they ventured through the city centre and would have been treated with short shrift during the mid-1960s had they made their presence felt at the ballrooms and larger dance halls whose audiences were, to a man and woman, working hard for the rest of the week. This was also true of some of the city bars.

It's hardly surprising, therefore, that the students would find their own venues such as The Maritime. It was a venue for variety-type concerts as well as trad jazz. On the ground floor, a café faced a flight of stairs, and along the narrow, institutional-like, painted passageway, there was a small dance hall. It had a low stage and bands would often walk through the audience to reach the stage, or, having finished their set, simply jump down from the stage and mill about with the crowd. They played short sets of half an hour to forty minutes, local band following local band; sometimes a visiting band would play. Belfast was very much part of the British circuit and most of the well-known and not so well-known bands of the time played the city.

The Maritime had, however, enough of its own bands to turn over two or three each night. They looked like their audiences and did whatever they fancied on stage, including smoking and drinking. The Maritime was breaking down the expected notion of musical entertainment as something that is 'provided by' an ensemble of musicians, and turning it into something that was created between the musicians and the audience.

There were no showband uniforms here or spangling glacial mirrors. The formal paired dancing of the ballrooms, even the riskier jive, gave way to solo expression, body to body, with a sexual frankness well beyond the sophisticated flirting and masquerade of showband music. No wonder I can recall the excitement of a friend's older sister telling us about this 'brilliant' dance club and then demurring in front of her mother about whether or not it would be a fit place for boys 'our age'. By the time we had moved into The Maritime, just after Them had broken up, it had become better known as Club Rado, but the name of The Maritime remained synonymous with excitement, risk and a sense of being part of a generation.

It was in actual fact an extraordinarily confined space with people crammed everywhere. Bands such as Sam Mahood and the Just Five religiously maintained the R & B ethos, while the slightly more college-based blues of The Few was clearly indebted to John Mayall, a regular visitor to the city with his Bluesbreakers, and the fervent soul of The Interns. Later on, Rory Gallagher and Taste played regularly at the club. Added to this 'tradition' of a few years' standing, bands whose showmanship often superseded their musical skills were eager to play at The Maritime, such as Arthur Brown's experience, who arrived on stage with a flaming headpiece to sing 'Fire'.

In April 1964, when Morrison and Them first played The Maritime, the atmosphere would have been significantly different because the band and audience were part of something that was new. The exhilaration of the music that Them played was part of the rejection of the established 'pop' music of the time, particularly in Ireland. Dublin had 'pop' and 'soul' bands, as indeed had Belfast. But Morrison's voice and Them's music, dress and mannerisms were guaranteed to satisfy a desire for rebellious self-assertion. The aggression is caught in the sound of the music; even when the song is of love lost, the regret is tinged with anger. Them played a style of R & B that was not only good to dance to but was also conscious of itself. Being a fan of Them, as well as listening to R & B for a generation, was subtly identifying oneself, and in the Belfast of that time, it carried the aura of being nominally 'anti-establishment', with The Maritime as the cavernous symbol.

The anthem of that identification was 'Gloria', the flipside of 'Baby, Please Don't Go', Them's second single, released in England in November 1964. The band had been playing for barely eight months but had a record in the British charts, and an appearance on the influential Independent Television's *Ready Steady Go!* programme. Confirmation of their status came with the decision to use 'Baby, Please Don't Go' as the programme's title music. With critical hindsight, Morrison's writing for 'Gloria' had found a perfect pitch: an aggressive and physical lyric that moves, literally step by step, towards sexual encounter. The almost martial drumming that Morrison breaks into with his story, 'like to tell you 'bout my baby', is urgent in its portrait of a midnight world:

> She comes walking down my street,
> Won't you come to my house
> She knocks upon my door
> And then she comes to my room
> Then she makes me feel alright.

The subjective territory of the song is stressed very much in the possessive – 'my' street, 'my' house, 'my' door and 'my' room. The link between street life and the inner sanctum is hypnotically cast as the girl's name is spelt out: G-L-O-R-I-A. Whatever about the speculations as to who 'Gloria' actually was (speculations which pursue many of Morrison's lyrics, most famously 'Madame George'), the focus is on the man and not the woman. That is what the shouting is all about. It is as if the singer was actually back on the street, calling; not uncommon in Belfast.

The echoey, sparse sound of 'Gloria' may well make it the first 'punk' record, as some maintain. For Morrison is, after all, writing out of a vibrant local idiom that prizes brash, almost confrontational, frankness. This did indeed involve calling out names and provocatively drawling vowels, like a summons to celebration. In the background of the song, the skipping tunes accompanying street games are not too far away from the emphatic rhythms, but they are transformed by the band from kid's stuff into passion. All the more important, therefore, to recall, by way of contrast, the tone of suburban ennui and middle-class complacency that sickens the young Gavin Burke in Brian Moore's highly regarded Belfast-based novel, *The Emperor of Ice Cream* (1965).

Set in Belfast of the 1940s, Moore's portrait of the city as 'this dull, dead town' remained a dominant cultural stereotype. Thwarted in love, disillusioned by narrow politics, put off by the self-consciously 'arty' set of his hometown, Gavin finds redemption only in the apocalyptic Blitz of the Second World War in which he (heroically) finds himself at last. In contrast, Sam Hanna Bell's *The Hollow Ball* (1961) tells a somewhat different kind of love story:

> They decided on a walk in the Botanic Gardens before going downtown. The sun dropping behind the Castlereagh Hills glittered on the pastel coats of the women, the starched collars of the respectable young men, the diamanté ornament in Maureen's fur collar. There was a tingle in the air that pierced their hands and turned their laughter to smoke. At the entrance to the new rose garden he caught her hand and they fled under the rustic arches, past the children and the dogs, past the gaping park attendant fumbling in his memory for a by-law that restrained young men and pretty girls from running in the winter sunlight, past the rude young men hooting at them from the shelter by the bandstand.

What Bell is hinting at here, and what his novel dramatises, are the ups and downs of life in Belfast. The important thing is that, according to Bell, there *was* an upside in the first place! The parks, the evening sunlight, the sexual joy and innocence, the music and, even though it is shadowed by that authority figure of the 'park attendant', the pronounced lyrical feeling of possibility. This is where Morrison comes in, with a vision all his own, conveyed through the exuberance of his voice.

With the demise of Them, after a time touring in England and in the States, Morrison's lyrics become preoccupied with what looks like a contradiction. For as Morrison discovers a rich thematic seam in writing about the Belfast he had grown up in, at the very same time, living in Belfast was frustrating him. 'As far as ideas and stuff were concerned,' he told Richie York, 'America was the place for me. That's the way it worked out ... For Belfast, my ideas were too far out.'

FIVE

Leaving Belfast in 1967 for New York, the twenty-one-year-old Morrison displayed not only tremendous courage but a forthright belief in his own artistic vision. As he remarked in an interview in 1987: 'All I did from the time I was eighteen to twenty-seven was work. I worked my way from Belfast to New York and didn't even know I was there because it was work.'

Like Bob Dylan leaving Hibbing, Minnesota, a decade earlier, Morrison was willing to use whatever he wanted to make up his own tradition out of diverse musical influences and try to forge a different kind of music. He displayed an iconoclastic individualism which, even to this day, has caused problems because it has to be sustained in the teeth of one of the most heartless and feckless of industries, the music industry. That confrontation is a key to understanding Morrison's lyrics – the battle for survival, aligned with his temperamental and critical reading of the media and pop culture; what he has called 'The Great Deception' and 'the fame game' that feeds off it. 'It all comes down to survival,' Morrison is quoted as saying in an interview with *Rolling Stone* (1990), 'and you can't intellectualise survival, because either you survive or you don't. That's the way life goes, and I'm not going to intellectualise it, because that's only going to spoil it.'

In 1968, having put behind him years of playing with several bands, from the Javelins and Monarchs to Them, working in Ireland, Scotland and England, touring Germany and America, Morrison made in *Astral Weeks* an imaginative repossession of his own past and the language and landscapes associated with it.

Much has been made about this early album of Morrison's; justly so. It is important, however, to remember that, like any performer, Morrison inhabits the stage as much as his work exists as recordings. The changing venues, musical contexts and audience expectations place the live performance in the realm of theatre, with the band as cast. As Morrison said, 'An album is roughly forty minutes of music, that's all.'

There is in Morrison's work the feeling that the lyrical sound is more important than the written song. The voice dominates what is sung because language turns into music at certain points; the tongue, the throat, the making of sound is its own instrument. Morrison was later to imitate pipe music as a mantra; an incantation that plays with the adequacy of language to convey feeling.

In *Astral Weeks* there is a sense of what Seán O'Hagan accurately calls Morrison's 'stretching the bounds of vocal expression to the limit'. This spontaneous yet experimental desire very much characterised the Beat Generation of the 1950s and early 1960s. Morrison came in contact with Jack Kerouac and Allen Ginsberg through his reading. The influence of Kerouac, along with Ginsberg and Gary Snyder, was, as the Beat Generation historian Anne Charters pointed out, central in linking poetry and jazz together in an attempted New Vision, tracking back to Blake and Walt Whitman, and also to Rimbaud and D.H. Lawrence.

In Morrison's situation, however, the controlling principle of his music is underscored by an inherited suspicion of artistic looseness. Morrison's poetic free form has never been excess but access; a contest between passion and restraint. Unlike the Beat poets' critique of American consumer culture, there is not the faintest interest in identifying alternative political or social mores in Morrison's writing. His songs are about rapture, not radicalism.

The eight tracks of *Astral Weeks*, recorded in two days in New York and released in the US in November 1968, present a reverie: a consistent personal dramatisation of mood, landscape, romantic longing and nostalgia for a lost Eden. *Astral Weeks* explores this earlier age of innocence, but the songs do so without sentimentalising the imagined past. The world of rivers, gardens, railway lines and particular avenues can be identified with Morrison's youth in east Belfast. The site of that past becomes emblematic, rather than being turned into local colour. Indeed, throughout *Astral Weeks*, as with Morrison's later albums, the naming of streets, districts and regions takes on an incantatory significance. The memory returns again and again to its first home as the alluring poetics of space, rather than the specific meaning of the place.

Astral Weeks is not the sudden breakthrough it has so often been described as; Morrison was, after all, working on this, and similar songs, in Belfast well before leaving for New York. More importantly, the main thrust of the songs remains close in theme and imagery to his earliest recorded work with Them: tracks such as 'Hey Girl', 'Philosophy' and, particularly, 'Friday's Child'. There is also the clear line that runs through his first recordings with Bert Berns for Bang Records, such as 'Joe Harper Saturday Morning' and 'The Back Room'.

The significant shift is in the musical treatment. It moved away from the hard-edged, probing 'group' sound with which Them channelled, indeed challenged, Morrison's voice. Instead the voice is articulated alongside the softer-focused, accoutisically led accompaniment. For the guitar (Jay Berliner), bass (Richard Davis), flute (John Payne), vibraphone (Warren Smith) and drums (Connie Kay of the Modern Jazz Quartet) all fuse into an orchestration of strings. What is produced is one continuous mood poem. Morrison's guitar might introduce the songs of *Astral Weeks*, but the poetic intention in his controlling voice is clear from the very beginning of the title track, 'Astral Weeks':

> To be born again, to be born again,
> To be born again, in another world darlin'

In another world.
In another time.

The desire in the voice, a hymn to love's possibility, picked out by the light touches of flute, strings and guitar, is guarded throughout *Astral Weeks* by a darker bass note that reminds us of uncertainty and vulnerability before Morrison laughs at himself at the song's end:

> Ain't nothin' but a stranger in this world,
> I'm nothin' but a stranger in this world,
> I got a home on high,
> In another land so far away, so far away.

The setting for *Astral Weeks* could not be simpler: two lovers, separated 'from the far side of the ocean', are joined together throughout these love songs. They walk through gardens and experience one another in a dream state. (An earlier, less coherent version of 'Beside You' depicts their encounter in explicitly physical terms, with the male figure dramatised in a much more forceful sense.)

While this untroubled world seems out of reach, the songs record the poet's own surroundings, with intriguing and sometimes obscure references:

> Little Jimmy's gone way out of the back
>   street,
> Out of the window, to the fog and rain,
> Right on time, right on time.

> That's why Broken Arrow waved his finger
>   down the road
> So dark and narrow,
> In the evening just before the Sunday six-
>   bells chime,
> Six-bells chime,
> And all the dogs are barking.

The city landscape is left behind as 'the country where the hillside mountains glide' comes into view, and in this Chagall-like transfiguration, the two young lovers meet, 'in the silence easy':

> You turn around, you turn around, you
>   turn around,
> You turn around, and I'm beside you,
>   beside you.

These love songs are all about an uncomplicated joy and the sense of release that singing his love's praises brings, troubadour fashion, as in 'Sweet Thing':

> And I will raise my hand up into the night
>   time sky,
> And count the stars that's shining in your
>   eye,
> Just to dig it all and not to wonder, that's
>   just fine,
> And I'll be satisfied not to read between
>   the lines.

The childlike love these songs court is of another time. In one of the best-known lyrics from *Astral Weeks*, 'Cyprus Avenue', Morrison reimagines the play between young lovers:

> You came walkin' down, in the wind and
>   rain, darlin',
> When you came walkin' down, the sun
>   shone through the trees
> And nobody can stop me from loving you,
>   baby.

There is, though, a further element introduced in 'Cyprus Avenue' as Morrison touches upon inarticulateness, that much-vaunted feature of Northern Irish cultural identity, and one that Morrison has explored (and made sport of) in live performances. In this instance, though, the issue is romantic (almost illicit) love. The expressiveness fights against itself, notwithstanding the Presley quotation, and tells a story of how difficult it is to say things to communicate powerful feelings:

> And my tongue gets tied
> Every, every, every time I try to speak
> And my insides shake just like a leaf on a tree.

What makes 'Cyprus Avenue' such an important song in Morrison's writing as a whole is the version of home that pervades it. Is that 'Mansion on the Hill' Stormont? It is barely a stone's throw from the actual

Cyprus Avenue. And is the railroad that disused railroad that runs nearby Holywood Arches, Bloomfield, Orangefield and Ballyhackamore? But what about those 'Six white horses on a carriage / Just returning from the Fair'? And what about that 'Yonder' – one of those words which live in Northern vernacular (as in 'Look at your man yonder') with an archaic literariness. Indeed, 'Cyprus Avenue' reads like an old English lyric but sounds like a Belfast street song. Between the formal poetry and the physical setting, Morrison's voice generates a troubled, robust ending amidst 'the avenue of trees'. In 'Cyprus Avenue' and the other songs from *Astral Weeks*, an imaginatively coherent image of Belfast emerges, particularly of course for those who grew up in the city.

The residential patterning of parts of the city, such as north and east Belfast, revealed a scallop shell of class segregation, not matched by other districts. Clustered around the lough on both shores, the working-class districts fanned out and upwards, via main arterial roads spliced with boulevard avenues, and often embracing distinctive districts that had once been villages, along with the new estates. The patterning incorporated rescheduled waterways, rivers and streams, as well as enclosing cemeteries, displaced big houses of once prosperous linen and shipping merchants, and maintained parks and green sites before reaching hillsides such as Castlereagh. This red-bricked civic landscape of back lanes ('entries'), streets, terraces, roads and avenues had a definite, if rarely articulated, class formation. To move within it was to experience the visible distinctions of a provincial, urban society. To move from it was to encounter the shifting magical thresholds between city and countryside. Morrison's songs are powerful testaments to both these levels of perception.

The mysterious luminous quality of *Astral Weeks* is earthed in the wonder, surprise and customs associated with leaving his own back bedroom, going down his own street ('as we said goodbye at your front door', he says in 'The Way Young Lovers Do') to inhabit his own district, its daylight and nightlight, walking through Beersbridge and Orangefield, taking everything in. Cyprus Avenue is not only a place, it is the idea of another place; the railway, the river: all are conduits through which Morrison's imagination is released.

'Madame George', the key song in *Astral Weeks*, dramatises this condition with a haunting portrait of belonging and leaving. This lyric, with its storytelling and repetitions, the anarchic mantra of 'the love' it seeks to express and its almost obsessive questioning, suggests comparison with the poet Patrick Kavanagh.

It is pure coincidence of course that Kavanagh, who was in the States in 1965 for a symposium on W.B. Yeats, should remark that he (Kavanagh) was all in favour of the Beat poets. 'I like Corso, Ferlinghetti, and Allen Ginsberg very much ... there are these lads in America, these youngsters that I admire very much.'

What Kavanagh saw in the work of the Beats is curious given the Irish situation he had in his mind. They had, he said, 'all written direct, personal statements, nothing involved, no, just statements about their position. That's all. They are not bores as far as I am concerned.' Kavanagh's dissatisfaction with convention ('boredom'), strengthened by his subjective romanticism ('direct personal statements'), is very close to the poetic vision of *Astral Weeks*, and in particular to the voice that recites 'Madame George'. I first heard the song early in 1969 from the US album, and by the time it was released in the UK in September of that year, *Astral Weeks* had achieved cult status.

Memory plays tricks with historical reality, but it seems to me, looking back to the twelve months between the end of 1969 and the close of 1970, that everyone was playing *Astral Weeks* throughout the Belfast I knew. That year was a watershed for every generation in Belfast, but particularly for those who were leaving their teenage years behind and becoming young men and women. Friends would soon go their own way, across the water to England, taking up jobs, going to college, and disappearing. The months leading out of the 1960s and into the 1970s correspond, loosely and in an inchoate, confused way, with a social and cultural break-up of life, as it had been known through the relative freedom of the preceding decade.

'Madame George' captured that feeling, and still does. It was a strange quiet before the storm. The clubs were still doing good trade, with parties at weekends, and visiting big names, such as Cream, Jimi Hendrix, Pink Floyd and The Small Faces, who all played the Ulster, King's or Whitla Hall. People hung out and there was little 'aggro', except for the usual sort of fighting that could make Belfast city centre a dangerous place on Saturday nights. But you could also walk throughout the wider city without too much anxiety or fear. Within a matter of a year, you would be taking your life in your hands for so doing. 'At an age when self-importance would have been normal,' remarked Philip Larkin of the 1940s, 'events cut us ruthlessly down to size'.

'Madame George' gives that freer time a distinctive sound and context. The shock of hearing the phrase 'On a train from Dublin up to Sandy Row' has never quite left me. An inexplicable connection, coded beneath the words themselves, identified for the first time the actual city in which I lived. Sandy Row, a Protestant working-class district in Belfast's inner city through which the train runs, is named; the custom of throwing pennies into the Boyne River (the iconographic 'Protestant' site of the eponymous battle), which we did without knowing why, and the transfixing 'trance' are all mentioned:

> Sitting on a sofa playing games of chance,
> With your folded arms in history books
>   you glance,
> Into the eyes of Madame George.

Much has been read into this extraordinary song. For me it is 'a child-like vision' which portrays a world of lost love, of ceremonies and evasions, past and present, shifting like a carousel between real and imagined people and places.

The soldier boy who is 'older now with hat on, drinking wine' – how many streets and roads had witnessed a few such men, tripping home after the pubs closed, at odds with the world they had returned to after the war; and the front rooms of their teenage children, 'filled with music / Laughing music, dancing music'?

'Madame George' is a portrait of a society about to withdraw from public view at the same time as the voice which describes it is also leaving the scene. Memories shift and coalesce. The site of the poem blurs and moves in and out of focus. It is the Belfast of Cyprus Avenue; there is a Fitzroy Avenue too. The rituals of 'collecting bottle-tops, going for cigarettes and matches in the shops' are identifiably Belfast. But the journey is on a train from Dublin *up to* Sandy Row; and there is a Fitzroy Avenue in Dublin.

Parsing the song in this fashion does not take us far. What is constant are the voices and the connections that Morrison makes between 'raps', 'cops', 'drops' and 'gots'. Quite simply, the song demonstrates what is truly unmistakable about Morrison's achievement – the steady, unflinching challenge which first his voice and then his lyrics and music embody. The voice is a powerful ambiguity, revelling in itself, but dismissive too, while the lyrics explore (and corroborate) much of the imaginative ambition and desire of Morrison's poetic peers.

Astral Weeks appeared in 1968, the same year as Derek Mahon's first poetry collection, *Night Crossing*. Around that year too, one sees a new and powerful generation of Northern Irish poets emerging out of the post-war period: Seamus Heaney, *Death of a Naturalist* (1966), *Door into the Dark* (1969); Michael Longley, *No Continuing City* (1969), with its 'Words for Jazz Perhaps' (updating Yeats); James Simmons, *Late But in Earnest* (1967) and *In the Wilderness* (1969); fellow east Belfast man Stewart Parker, *The Casualty's Meditation* (1966), *Maw: A Journey* (1968) (and whose 'High Pop' column in *The Irish Times* hailed Morrison's albums with bright intelligence and insight).

Like other Irish artists before him, Morrison's move to America was a liberating one at the time. The albums that followed *Astral Weeks – Moondance* (1970), *His Band & the Street Choir* (1970), *Tupelo Honey* (1971), *St Dominic's Preview* (1972), *Hard Nose the Highway* (1973) – are an imagining of America and the extraordinary sense of freedom (as well as obsessiveness) associated with the place. As John Wilson Foster remarked about his own upbringing in east Belfast during the 1940s and early 1950s, 'We grew up steeped in American popular culture. America was the fourth country we lived in.' It was all part of an extraordinary, potent mix. So the 'years of hope', which Jonathan Bardon described as the period between 1945 and 1968, etched themselves indelibly in the emotional, cultural and political experience of an entire generation. Morrison gives voice to the hope and excitement, the energy and drive, shadowed by the knowledge of loss and pain.

SIX

During my teens, much of my time outside school hours at Belfast's Orangefield, and often inside them as well, was spent going to clubs, dances and concerts in Belfast's city centre. At night, and sometimes twice daily on Wednesdays and Saturdays, a group of friends met at the Wimpy Bar, the Athletic Stores or on the steps of the Linen Hall Library. We went to Sammy Houston's Jazz Club, Betty Staffs, The Maritime, The Rikki Tikki Club, Inst., The Floral Hall, The Orpheus, The Fiesta or King George Hall. A large chunk of our lives was devoted to listening to music, dancing to it and buying it. Music was our life and Belfast was full of it: R & B, blues, folk, rock, jazz and pop.

But beyond all the other remarkable home-based bands and singers that played Belfast, the voice and lyrics of Van Morrison record an extraordinary range and focus. The individualism of the man is totally at one with the city he grew up in and has returned to consistently in his work. By the time he had left (1967), Morrison had already been working as a musician for several years, initially playing at local cinemas and school 'hops' before making what used to be called 'The Charts' with Them in the mid-1960s. Since then

Morrison has established himself not only as a dominant figure in the shifting sands of the music business but, much more importantly, in the wider world beyond. His work inhabits a fascinating imaginative space which has continuously moved in and out of his audience's expectations. It has to do with the way he sings as much as with what he sings; a critical state of mind.

At the very heart of his work, there is a series of dilemmas. Morrison has spoken of these in the interviews he has given throughout his career; they reveal Morrison as a vastly experienced and uncompromising critic of the contemporary world and the fate within it of genuine artistic endeavour.

As a musician, all Morrison needs to do is entertain (what he calls 'earning my living'), but there is also a profound desire to communicate more than that; as a performer, there is the conflict between protecting the individual private self while dealing with the mass-market music business that thrives on and exploits disclosure.

So when we sat on the darkened stage to chat publicly at the Closing Festival of the UK Year of Literature and Writing in Swansea in 1995, the two worlds came together, with an audience that wasn't too sure what to expect, other than to hear something about Morrison's views on writing.

Not known for public conversation, it seemed we were on a hiding to nothing. Yet, listening again to the taped recording, Morrison was actually quite revealing and frank:

VM: I hadn't a clue what Yeats's 'Before the World Was Made' was about.

GD: Mystical?

VM: Mystical is just another word. Spiritual is a word. I don't think it's a word. I think it's some kind of energy and I don't think anyone knows what the energy is. These words were made up to describe some kind of energy.

He spoke about his admiration for the Belfast novelist Brian Moore, and also about his sense of being on the tail end of the 1950s generation, when writers like Kerouac, whose *Dharma Bums* Morrison had read in his arty teens, had 'opened things up'. It was 'an inspiring period with a different landscape'. He also spoke of how the Beat Generation had, in turn, been influenced by French writers and by Joyce. The interconnectedness between writing and music was apparent at every turn of phrase and at each halting hesitation.

GD: Where does your writing come from?

VM: Sometimes you get a title; people, places, streets. There's no set thing; it's a mishmash and fragmented. Later on you piece it together, in retrospect: poetry and songs are basically all the same thing.

GD: Was there any one song that changed your direction?

VM: Yes, the second version of 'Astral Weeks'. I re-did it all and it became a direction. Some songs I'm doing tonight I haven't done for ten years and more. Twenty years in fact.

The second part of the evening was given over to the songs, and was vintage Morrison unplugged. It included a magnificent 'Madame George' and 'The Healing Game'. Backed by the impeccable Georgie Fame and the young band, which features on the *How Long Has This Been Going On* album, Morrison set the wintry Welsh evening on fire. It must have been one of his most spellbinding performances.

Directed by Derry man Seán Doran, alongside a team that included Liam Brown, the UK Year of Literature attracted just under 1,000 writers to take part in nearly 500 events. They included Nobel laureates Kenzaburō Ōe and Seamus Heaney, together with Jane Smiley, Alison Lurie, Rita Dove and a host of other writers, such as Allen Ginsberg, Sorley MacLean, David Lodge, Brian Keenan and James Kelman. Together they made the Welsh city the scene of the largest literature festival ever staged.

I had already attended the UK Year of Literature and Writing earlier that year for an event called 'The Importance of Being Elsewhere', devoted to writers from Ireland. Ciaran Carson and I gave a reading and talked about how Belfast, the city we grew up in, had influenced our writing. As for the tangible legacies of the festival itself, the organisers left behind them Ty

Lien, a national literature centre for Wales, the first purpose-built centre of its kind in the UK.

For me, however, the festival will be indelibly fixed by the image of Van Morrison on stage with his band, though in his mind he was in some other place, the archetypal Hyndford Street:

> And voices echoing late at night
> Over Beechie River
> And it's always being now
> And it's always being now
> It's always now
> Can you feel the silence?

GD: We were talking in Dublin on Saturday and you mentioned to me where some of the lines come from, way back. You mentioned one very well-known song, 'Mystic Eyes', and you mentioned the fact that it actually came from *Great Expectations*.

VM: We saw *Great Expectations* on TV when I was about twelve. 'Mystic Eyes' has an image of a graveyard in it, which was inspired by the graveyard scene in *Great Expectations*.

GD: Are there many poems that have come that way?

VM: Inspiration for poems or songs can come from anywhere, from things people say, books, magazines, conversations, dreams. There is no set format.

GD: What was the first poem you wrote?

VM: I wrote it when I was still at school, at about thirteen or fourteen. It was about the dinner-time atmosphere, the smells, the sounds that I was picking up as the men (including my father) were coming home from working at the shipyard. It has since been lost.

GD: Did you ever think of publishing that stuff?

VM: At one point, I did have a book of material going way back, but it was never published.

GD: What about some of the things like your father's collection of books, those Wild West stories?

VM: Yes, I used to read my father's jazz books and some of his Wild West stories.

GD: And, of course, all around him then was all the R & B and blues?

VM: Well, he was mainly into New Orleans jazz and blues.

GD: You listened to that all the time?

VM: Yes, that's where I heard the music first.

GD: Where was the feed line into writing, to actually write a poem, to read a book? That didn't come from Orangefield, the school you went to?

VM: No, it didn't actually, because we didn't get to read many books then except some Shakespeare once. We weren't taught about any Irish writers.

GD: Who was the first poet that came your way that you remember?

VM: The first poetry book that I had was a compilation of various poets, though I can't remember the title of this book.

GD: Was Yeats one of them?

VM: I didn't come across Yeats until later on, in the seventies, when I discovered that he had written a series of poems called 'Words for Music Perhaps'. I compared a few of my songs to Yeats's songs. Then I started reading more about him and his work.

GD: People make connections between you and Yeats and about the sense of mystery and so on. You were actually thinking about this way before you ever read Yeats? There was no connection—

VM: I'd probably written about a hundred songs before I read any Yeats.

GD: And was that the kind of stuff you were doing then, were they all based around Belfast? Were those lyrics, those early lyrics, like from *Astral Weeks* or even from stuff you were doing with Them, they were all coming out of east Belfast?

VM: Some of my writing was autobiographical with Them, like 'The Story of Them' and some others. But then some of it was American R & B. It's always been a mixture.

GD: The one book that I keep on hearing people talk about when they talk about your lyrics is Jack Kerouac's *On the Road*. Did you feel that that was liberating in some way?

VM: I was just coming in on the tail end of the fifties generation of people. I think that book really opened up people's minds. In fact, he opened up the whole sixties freedom vibe.

GD: It just opened up 'what'?

VM: Well, he opened up the spontaneity of ideas and writing in general. He was the spearhead of the Beat poetry movement that included poets like Ginsberg, Ferlinghetti, Corso and Burroughs.

GD: And that stuff was around Belfast at the time? You were picking up that vibe in Belfast. It was before you went to London ...

VM: Yes, a friend of mine introduced me to him. *Dharma Bums* was the first book of his that I read. He gave me a copy of it when I was thirteen or fourteen.

GD: And you just said, 'I want to write like this'?

VM: No, not really, it was just inspiring as a period. It wasn't just writing; it was ideas, and it was coming out in films. It was just a different landscape.

GD: When you say films, we're talking about what, James Dean, Marlon Brando, because they're in the songs?

VM: Yes, Marlon Brando's films and things like that.

GD: Again the notion of these guys on their own, doing their own thing, breaking away from the places where they're known.

VM: I thought that perhaps Kerouac was influenced by people before him like French writers, James Joyce, and maybe Kenneth Patchen.

GD: But was there any sense in Belfast, you never felt that you were a writer, you never felt that you were part of any literary thing; it was just music, wasn't it? You didn't really feel that you were a Belfast writer.

VM: No, because I hadn't been educated about any literary traditions; there was little taught on this subject during the late fifties and early sixties in Belfast. I have spoken to people who went to school in Dublin at this time and they said the same: they didn't receive that type of education either. It seems like it wasn't cool or whatever to teach young school children about literary traditions during the period I was in school.

GD: Do you think that in some way music was your way through, and then you started to write songs, lyrics? Did you ever see yourself as being a poet first and then a songwriter second, or was it all just one thing you were doing?

VM: I never thought about it that much, but some of what I wrote could be termed as just poetry. At some point, I usually turn some of this poetry into songs. But I have also some poetry which I keep as poetry.

GD: Like an idea in the back of the head that you were writing a ballad. Had you some kind of frame in the back of your head or did you just write the stuff out?

VM: Well, with me, a lot of it is unconscious. It's only later on that I may be able to piece the connections or inspiration together.

GD: You saw where you were coming from?

VM: Yes, in retrospect.

GD: You have written a lot of songs, poems with a Scottish influence, and then there is the connection with Kavanagh. Is there a sense in which you feel part of the ballad tradition, troubadours and balladeers, rather than being a poet?

VM: It's really all the same. The difference is you just do it with music.

GD: What about Blake and that marvellous version that you have of 'Let the Slave' and 'The Price of Experience?'. Where did that come from? What drew you there?

VM: I first heard this piece by Blake being performed on a record by Mike Westwood. But I'd been reading Blake for a while before that. This was the first time though that I had heard him put to music. So I just did my own version of it.

GD: Do you carry songs in your head for a while, or lyrics in your head and then write them down or ... how does it click?

VM: Sometimes I get a title and then just make a note of it. Then I sometimes get a whole line or a couple of lines and make a note of them. It can go on from there; I work on it when I get it. If I get stuck, I come back to it later. So it can be a mish-mash, and very fragmented at times. Then on the other hand, some songs and poems come all together in a flow. This is what Yeats referred to as automatic writing. It is my favourite form of inspiration and writing. An example of this is 'Summertime in England'.

GD: But the last five or six albums are drawn toward east Belfast – the river, the church bells, there's a certain language you seem to be excited by, and keep on going back toward, almost as if it's like a womb that you are going back to, an image that you keep on having to go back and touch. Does that happen – the sense that you want to go back there and make connections?

VM: Yes, I suppose so.

GD: It happens that particular landscape is where you're drawn?

VM: I don't know if it's landscape; it might be just people, places, it might be streets.

GD: The reason why I'm asking you [is] that lyric that we were talking about earlier on, the Yeats lyric – we seem to keep coming back to Yeats, the one you recorded, 'Before the World was Made' – with the line, 'I'm looking for the face I had before the world was made / What if I look upon you now. As though on my beloved / And my blood be cold the while. And my heart unmoved'. You know the way that in so many of the poems you [have] this extraordinary sense of the simple statement. It's very absolute, it's clear.

VM: Yeah, it's slightly different, isn't it? Well, what intrigued me about this is that I hadn't a clue what it was about. And because people ask me, 'Do you know what's it's about?' – about my own work, I can relate to that. There are times, I don't know what my work is about; I haven't a clue. Yeats must have known what this work was about or, then again, maybe he didn't know either.

GD: He was chancing it as well?

VM: Yeah, probably.

GD: Do you want to give us a few—

VM [reads]:
'If I paint the lashes dark
And the eyes more bright
And the lips more scarlet
Or ask if all be right
From mirror after mirror
No vanity's displayed:
I'm looking for the face I had
Before the world was made.'

GD: It has got that extraordinary simplicity about it though.

VM: It all depends on what he means by the world was 'made'.

GD: Did you feel that there's always going to be these dark, grey, uncertain areas in everything that Yeats or Blake writes, and this sense of rapture, of ecstasy, that sense of another world that you are trying to make contact with a mystical thing?

VM: Well, I don't know if it's mystical. To me, 'mystical' is just another loaded word, like the word 'spiritual'. But I don't think this sense that you refer to can be described in a word. I think that it's some sort of unknown energy. It may have been photographed with Kirlian photography. Therefore, these words 'mystical' and 'spiritual' are describing some sort of energy, and maybe some sort of vision as well.

GD: And poetry's part of that?

VM: Yeah, I think so.

GD: Poetry's the most important part for you.

VM: Well, it's the energy. It might be a poem or a song, or it might be an instrumental without words, but it's all the same energy that is invoked.

GD: Who would you think – Paul Durcan has worked with you and you're drawn toward certain energies in what he does. Kavanagh's there, Yeats is there. Blake's there. What is the significance for you of America? That's in the freedom of Kerouac and so on?

VM: Well, that was when I was a kid before I lived in America. But when I lived there, it was a whole different thing. Kerouac himself didn't really want to know about America.

GD: I'm trying to draw you on this notion of America ... Did America provide you with a kind of space, or an imagined place, somewhere totally different than Belfast?

VM: Yes, but I mean Kerouac was writing about an America of the imagination, not a real America.

GD: And does Ireland provide you with stuff like that? You know, you go back—

VM: Well, it's like I said, it's different people. Sometimes I read Brian Moore. I remember reading about ten of his books in a row one time – because that was the connection at that time. Do you know what I am saying?

GD: That there's somebody who happens at one moment and then you get into that work and read all of it and then you move on to something else.

VM: No, you might not move on. You could move on, then come back to it. Moore writes about that connection that you're taking about, like Belfast, et cetera. Because he always goes back, to Belfast, at least once a year, but he doesn't stay.

GD: He's out there in the States too. What about this thing you often hear talk about – the 'Celtic Fringe' – you were doing this for a long time before it became very popular, plugging into Celtic energy. Do you feel that that's very important for you, that you're Irish, that you're from that kind of background? Does that really mean a lot to you, that you can identify with what's going in Scotland, Wales, or further?

VM: I think there's some sort of Celtic energy, but I think that everywhere is being taken over by the twenty-first century. So, I think that you have really to go to remote places, to experience the spiritual level or whatever of it. I don't know if this energy level still exists. I think it was a reality a long, long time ago, but now I think that it's maybe just part of the imagination.

GD: It's accepted now. It's become bureaucratic almost. It doesn't have any kind of real punch anymore. Is that what you are saying?

VM: No, I'm saying that this identification thing is very commercial, as we ... as everything else ... so you don't know what's real and what isn't.

GD: Going back through all the lyrics you have written – 220 of them now – which one or two do you think are important statements that have really changed your direction when you wrote them? Is there any one in particular?

VM: I don't think so. When I perform, I work out a set that my band learns. But some of the older songs I come back to, I'm doing some songs tonight that I haven't done for maybe ten years or more. Some of them I haven't probably done for twenty years, so I don't really know.

GD: So there's not one or two that stand out in your mind – when you wrote them you said to yourself, 'That has taken me into some other kind of area, I've changed my kind of direction having written that'?

VM: Well, yes, there's *Astral Weeks*; that was the one that changed the direction for me.

GD: You mean the lyric itself as distinct to the album?

VM: Well, the lyric and the music and the whole direction, because that was the second time I recorded it. I recorded it for the first time with a producer who hadn't a clue what the songs were about or what the music was about, so I redid it all, and then that became a new direction for me.

GD: And I often think that in *Hymns to the Silence* there is a resolved statement in those songs, a very clear idea about what they were saying. You're going to do 'On Hyndford Street' this evening. The other one that I was thinking about was your short story 'Boffyflow and Spike'. Would you read a bit of that for us?

VM: Why don't you read some of it? I think that you might be a better reader than me. I could play guitar while you read it maybe.

[VM picks up the guitar]

[GD reading, accompanied by VM]:
'So let us follow Boffyflow and Spike down through the days of the leaves. Boffy is covered with leaves completely, the buckeejit, and Spike is in hysterics. On they go, on and on up the small incline, gathering sacks of leaves for burning in the clearing and waiting for McDole.

'McDole has not been seen nor heard of since Halloween and everyone is getting a trifle nervous. Spike took the sheet of paper from his inside coat pocket and tried to decipher the code, but as he glanced over the page, he realised he had not noticed the note in the margin that said "It means what it means," followed by, "Wee Alfie at the Castle picture house on the Castlereagh Road, whistling on the corner next door where he kept Johnny Mack Brown's horse. 'O Sole Mio' by McGimsey and the man who played the saw outside the City Hall. Pastie suppers down at Davy's Chipper, gravy rings, barmbracks, wagon wheels, snowballs. A Sense of Wonder."'
[1985]

GD: Could you do that one? This is the one that we were talking about at the beginning. It seems extraordinary that this song, which has gone throughout the world – everybody thinks it's about something else – that it actually comes out of *Great Expectations*.

VM: Well, just the imagery ... I would also need a full band to perform it as it's all R & B.

GD: Well, will you not even just read it so the audience will know what we are talking about. [VM sings with guitar]

VM [singing with guitar]:
'One Sunday morning,
We went walking
Down by the old graveyard
In the morning fog
And looked into those mystic eyes
Mystic eyes, mystic eyes, mystic eyes, mystic eyes
Mystic eyes, mystic eyes, mystic eyes, mystic eyes.'

SEVEN

When am turns to was and now is back when,
Will someone have moments like this,
Moments of unspoken bliss?

–Mose Allison, 'Was'

Writing and performing his work since the early 1960s, Morrison takes his audience on a unique journey. From Belfast city streets and the surrounding countryside to the London of Camden Town, Tottenham Court Road, Notting Hill Gate and Ladbroke Grove, to New York, California and other American locations and to various European cities, such as Paris and Geneva; Morrison's writing has no destination. These poems, folk and love songs, ballads, hymns and blues, explore universal themes that have marked Van Morrison since the very beginning as a solitary figure; a stranger in this world. Morrison grew up in east Belfast's mainly Protestant working-class neighbourhood, though his own family was not deeply religious.

The district, and in particular areas such as Orangefield, nestled under the magical Castlereagh Hills, is within easy reach of the north Down coastline, with its resorts and fishing villages dotted along Belfast

Lough, from Holywood, along the Irish Sea, to the stunning mountains of Mourne. Much of Morrison's writing carries this landscape within it.

The Belfast that Morrison grew up in, the post-war era of the 1950s and 1960s, no longer exists, as the economic life that underpinned its energies and lifestyle was already disappearing by the early 1970s. By then Morrison had left the city of his childhood and young manhood and was establishing a reputation for himself in America as one of the most exacting and exciting singer-song writers of his time and generation. The journey for the young Morrison took him from being the lead singer with Them to becoming a critically acclaimed artist in his own right, beginning with two Bang Records albums, and followed by *Astral Weeks*. It is a story, told many times before, but never better than in Morrison's own words. The sense of leaving the familiar and known, the home place, to find a sustaining artistic life elsewhere, is scored throughout Morrison's work from the beginning, in 'The Back Room': 'You gotta go out there and do something for yourself'.

The world that is left behind is depicted in emotional, physical and (at times) ironic detail. The Spanish Rooms, Lower Falls, Belfast, was, for instance, a well-known 'haunt' of the 1960s, famous for its 'scrumpy', an intoxicating cider – as Morrison recounts in 'The Story of Them': 'Four pints of that stuff was enough to have you out of your mind'. Close by was The Maritime, the dance club with which Morrison and Them had become synonymous. Life on the road, moving from room to room with little money, is etched in his writing of this time: both the excitement and the insecurity. Yet the early writing also records Morrison's growing unease and detachment. What he eventually took with him proved to be, with his talent and application, one of the greatest sources of his creative inspiration.

For not only were these memories of a life shared with family and friends but also of the sounds, rhythms and nuances of the way Belfast people talk. The very accent was a sign of belonging. So Morrison's lyrics are suffused with the verbal tone and inflection of his native city. He hones all the proverbial wit, the aphoristic questioning, the emotional and physical directness, the taunting mockery and self-reliance into an accurate and vivid recreation of spoken English. Time and again, he catches the precise turn of phrase with which an idea, an emotion, an image, is revealed. And spurned as well. 'My back was up against the wall'; 'When push comes to shove'; 'I've been through the mill!'; 'Just as long as I fit the bill'; 'Put your money where your mouth is'. The sounds and meanings of local idioms course through his writing with such unselfconscious conviction that they are a joy in themselves. Morrison hears the way people speak in many different, sometimes simultaneous, registers. This ability lends his expression its utterly distinctive intensity: the repetitions, the abbreviations and the ad libs; they reflect the unpunctuated feeling of how people actually say things and share feelings. Alongside the chastening frankness and romantic honesty of the writing ('You make me feel so free', 'Have I told you lately that I love you?'), there is also an impatience with language, that it can let you down and be insufficient to the task of expressing love or spirituality. 'Listen to the music inside. Can't you hear what it says to you?' This is perhaps why Morrison was drawn so early to Celtic fables and folklore, from Avalon to Tír na nÓg, as a way of sourcing different kinds of emotional reality.

From the streets, corners and backyards of home to the intimacies of passion, love, separation and loss, Morrison's writing creates its own landscape. The garden, the river, the railway nearby (the 'viaducts of your dreams'), where he grew up and, continually, the street ('You can't be complete without a street'), avenue (such as the original Cyprus Avenue, 'the avenue of trees') and road all are symbolically recovered, along with the voices and names of friends, lovers and places that belong to that recurring past. So, too, with some of the old customs of a disappearing way of life which Morrison had once lived and known so well: the key in the letter box, the kids playing rhyming songs, skipping home from school, the late-night chat on the window sill, the pre-eminence of the radio (Voice of America, Radio Luxembourg, BBC Third Programme), Morrison's lyrics are literally full of this life, in retrospect; a weaving of now and then. The musical form, which captures this sense of a lost time and of new beginnings, is the blues. As Morrison remarked, what he likes to do is 'sing the blues and that's what I do best'.

Throughout his writing the hints of other songs ('shaking like a leaf') and idioms ('fair play to you', 'the craic was good'), along with song titles, echo with their own fascinating refrain. Such openness makes Morrison's writing alive to the everyday and the way in which people will unselfconsciously quote song standards and euphemisms as a way of saying (or not saying) things. Indeed this playfulness and ironic humour ('taking the piss') is far too often overlooked in relation to Morrison. Interpretations that are overly serious, miss out on the fun, for some of the energy of his writing and, naturally, his performances comes from the enjoyment Morrison experiences playing music and making contact with his audience, in spite of the crude caricatures that prevail and imply the contrary. As he has said elsewhere, 'There have been many good times and craic right throughout my life and work from the early days to the present.'

Morrison delves into the unnamed and unnamable sense of wonder ('paradise') that comes with his feeling for nature and lost innocence. A 'new' world always beckons, rapturous and trance-like, which defies definition and is transcendental: 'the eternal now'. This romantic longing and self-dramatisation goes beyond language as the very sound of a word, its acoustic, is probed, along with the anatomy of a cliché or the simplest of memories – cleaning windows, shovelling snow away, or in the poignant reimagining of his father 'chopping wood'. All are turned into a different kind of experience: 'The words we do not need to speak'. The bright side of this writing can be at times shadowed by a darker view – of mortality, exile, and (increasingly) of Morrison's reaction to the draining falseness of 'celebrity' and the overriding priorities of a contemporary culture that is much more concerned with marketing than with music; with style rather than with substance; with 'too many myths'. The stark recognition of his predicament in relation to these illusions and myths highlights the priorities of our time: the short-circuiting of real life within the fatuous 'ship of fools' and fame, 'that monkey on my back'. Yet quite early on, Morrison saw the 'Great Deception' of the music business as antipathetic to true artistic independence and the values of human communication, with its cut-throat commercial preoccupations and amnesiac hype: 'No one says what they mean'. He saw the hypocrisies involved as well: 'Rock and roll singers got three or four Cadillacs saying power to the people' while the 'so-called hippies ... take the eyeballs straight out of your head'. He has written of the inner turmoil such a way of life inevitably brings in its wake: 'If this is success then something's awful wrong' cause I bought the dream and I had to play along.' Dealing with the 'Big-time Operators' becomes a battle for survival:

> They were glorified by the media
> They were heroes who had names
> They said that they would bury me
> If I didn't play their game.

Against this, the individual talent has to find some kind of balance and self-respect: 'All I ever wanted was simply just to be me'. Morrison describes the meaning and cost of such a growing consciousness and what turns out to be a moral struggle for self-worth and artistic values, something which younger contemporaries might take note of.

This disillusioned and, at times, acerbic strain in Morrison's writing contrasts with the ongoing energy he associates with those artists, writers and musicians of the past whom he clearly honours and reveres: William Blake, W.B. Yeats, Jack Kerouac, Huddie Ledbetter, Ray Charles, Mahalia Jackson, Hank Williams, Jimmie Rodgers, Muddy Waters, Sonny Terry, Brownie McGhee, Lightnin' Hopkins, Sonny Boy Williamson and, particularly, John Lee Hooker. Others can be added, others whose names have either passed from public view in the rapid, 'history-less' commercialism of today, or who carry on, playing their music, performing their songs, writing their work beyond the gaze of the media and the 'name game'.

Underpinning Morrison's work of the 1980s and 1990s is a deepening philosophical understanding of the world; an existential 'aloneness', the unavoidable loneliness against which his writing and his music is both a cry of the heart and a rage. In, for instance, 'What's Wrong with this Picture?' Morrison freely speaks his mind, not only about a lost and irretrievable past, but also about what he sees as present human folly:

You can't believe what you read in the papers
Or half the news that's on TV
Or the gossip of the neighbours
Or anyone who doesn't want to be free.

I'm not that person anymore
I'm always living in the present time
Don't you understand
I left all that jive behind.

He reprises the classical injunction, 'I just wanna get on with the show', with the perfectly pitched irony: 'Nero fell while Rome burnt / Napoleon met his Waterloo / Samson went spare when Delilah cut his hair / But little David slew Goliath too'. Over the years of his life in music, Morrison has probed the boundaries where blues, jazz, R & B, folk, traditional music and poetry merge. His strongly rooted sense of musicality, of the repertoire of songs and melodies, of making music, underscores the wider, lonelier, instinctive stretches of his own writing. Out of these extraordinarily diverse influences – musical, literary, cultural, philosophical and mystical – he has moulded his own tradition, as image borrows image in an unfolding poetic narrative that cross-references music, song, jazz and poetry into a singular and lasting achievement.

Albert Camus once remarked, 'At least I know with sure and certain knowledge that a man's work is nothing but this slow trek to rediscover through the detours of art those two or three great and simple images in whose presence his heart first opened.' Van Morrison's lyrics tell the story of this rediscovery with a rare intensity and vision.

In his August 1972 'High Pop' column for *The Irish Times*, Stewart Parker wrote his review of Van Morrison's *Saint Dominic's Preview*:

Belfast should name a street after Van Morrison. Of all the hard men from the industrial provinces of these islands who made their names during the 1960s by imitating black R & B singers, he alone has gone on to fulfil his promise ... He has done it through perseverance, determination, steady toil: so a city that has always prided itself on its Puritan work-ethic could scarcely find a worthier off-spring to honour.

Belfast – 'The streets that I came from', as Morrison has it – honoured Ivan George Morrison with the freedom of the city in 2013, and three years later he was knighted for his musical achievements and his services to tourism and charitable causes in Northern Ireland. Morrison is respected, indeed revered, in many cities and countries throughout North America, Europe, and even farther afield. His standing as a singer-songwriter has been well established since he stepped outside the community of the various bands he played in as a young musician. But as Parker knew well, there was much more to this familiar story:

The singing is only a part of Morrison's music. He is an artist who has gradually achieved control over all the components of his material – he writes the songs, orchestrates and produces them. The result is an entirely distinctive sound which is always unmistakably his own.

With the publication of *Lit Up Inside: Selected Lyrics* in 2014, the reader of poetry can see what Parker was getting at all those years ago, because Morrison's lyrics, selected here by fellow Belfast man Eamon Hughes, carry within them the conviction of a spiritual journey, although one that should bear Morrison's own caveat: 'Pay the Devil'.

These lyrics are witnesses to love gained and lost and to a search for home as the poignancy of childhood and innocence is viewed through the realities of hard-earned experience. Throughout Morrison's writing – in the language of street song and declaimed literary allusion, the rhythms of ballad bolstered with the throwaway lines of local speech – the yearning poet's voice seeks to recapture a past that is cast within the most emblematic of inner-city landscapes and harbours of voyage. Ship foghorns echo like dream songs, as do the misty gardens and magical secret places of adolescence – from the back room to street corners – all are recalled as memories, physically voiced on stage and represented now in these pages, as artful expressions of simply being here:

Look at the ivy on the old clinging wall
Look at the flowers and the green grass so tall
It's not a matter of when push comes to shove
It's just the hour on the wings of a dove
It's just warm love, it's just warm love.

The lyrical beat of repetition, the imploring questions, the injunctions, matter a lot because of the spokenness of *Lit Up Inside*. These songs of innocence and experience are addressed to someone, and by the time the lyric has entered the mainstream, it is 'you' and 'I' who are doing the talking. At stake too there are songs of emigration – 'Celtic Ray' a perfect example – and the inside story of 'the show business' and its 'rat race' finds no clearer expression than 'The Great Deception' or 'Why Must I Always Explain?'

There is a kind of mini-history within *Lit Up Inside*, a condensed version of how a particular time survives in the poet's mind, revealing in 'Wild Children' some of the post-Second World War names of the great transatlantic popular culture in which Morrison's generation was immersed – Tennessee Williams, Rod Steiger, Marlon Brando, James Dean, a host of musicians like Sidney Bechet, but also including the famous Beat Generation of Jack Kerouac, name-checked elsewhere alongside Beckett and Joyce. And in 'Summertime in England' and 'Rave On, John Donne', playful cascading litanies to the joy of simply living ('It just is, that's all there is about it'), Morrison stretches the line of meaning to exclamation, and the incantatory point of his performance:

> Did you ever hear about, did you ever hear about
> Wordsworth and Coleridge
> Smokin' up in Kendal?

These trance-like, free-forming lyrics are amazing, for there is little in contemporary music with which to compare, say, 'Burning Ground' or the earlier 'Madame George', with its dramatised epiphany of farewell:

> When you fall into a trance
> Sitting on a sofa playing games of chance
> With your folded arms and history books
>   you glance
> Into the eyes of Madame George.

But what stays in the heart and soul of Morrison's selected lyrics is the revelatory images of 'Brand New Day', the portrait of his father in 'Choppin' Wood', the remarkable hymns to family life in 'On Hyndford Street', the drifty, unmoored mantra of 'Take Me Back', the transcendent simplicity of 'Have I Told You Lately That I Love You?', the joyful reveal in 'The Way Young Lovers Do' or the upbeat uncomplicated praise of 'Moondance':

> Well, it's a marvellous night for a moondance
> With the stars up above in your eyes
> A fantabulous night to make romance
> 'Neath the cover of October skies.

In common with the great 'anti-phony' Patrick Kavanagh, whose lyrical grace Morrison resembles at times, the characteristic walking down familiar streets in search of that elusive, authentic past finds an utterly unique and mischievously vernacular rendering in 'Cleaning Windows':

Oh the smell of the bakery from across the street
Got in my nose
As we carried our ladders down the street
With the wrought-iron gate rows
I went home and listened to Jimmie Rodgers
In my lunch break
Bought five Woodbine at the shop on the corner
And went straight back to work.

Oh Sam was up on top
And I was on the bottom with the V
We went for lemonade and Paris buns
At the shop and broke for tea
I collected from the lady
And I cleaned the fanlight inside out
I was blowing saxophone on the weekend
In a Down joint.
What's my line?
I'm happy cleaning windows.

'Cleaning Windows' is an unexpected reminder of just how much living and working has gone into the making of Morrison's writing, and on the road, in the other places his work has taken him, from Somerset and London to California and Canada, Geneva and Scandinavia. But the talismanic Orangefield of east Belfast is at the heart's core, with its 'Sunday six bells' and:

Going up the Castlereagh Hills and the
Cregagh Glens

> In summer and coming back
> To Hyndford Street, feeling wondrous and
>   lit up inside.

Van Morrison's glorious art, for which these lyrics are the score, comes close to perfection with 'In the Garden', which opens, as if for the very first time, with his own confounded ecstatic recollection, since that 'always' is complicated with an emotional understanding that means much more than remembrance:

> The fields are always wet with rain
> After a summer shower
> When I saw you standing, standing in the
>   garden
> In the garden, wet with rain.

ACKNOWLEDGEMENTS

The book is developed from all the material I have published on Van Morrison since the early 1990s.

Acknowledgements are kindly made to Marian Richardson, Clíodhna Ní Anluain, Adrian Rice, Mel McMahon, Rev. Gary Hastings, Kevin Smith, David Gardiner, Caroline Walsh, Jonathan Williams, Patrick Ramsey, James Kerr (Lagan/Verbal Arts), Jonathan Dykes and Fintan O'Toole. Extracts from this book were originally broadcast on RTÉ and BBC Northern Ireland and also published in *The Irish Times*, *Fortnight*, *Review of Irish Studies*, *The Rest is History* (1998), subsequently collected in *My Mother-City* (2007), *The World as Province* (2009) and *Conversations: Poets & Poetry* (2011). The interview with Van Morrison was part of the UK Year of Literature and took place in the Brangwyn Hall, Swansea, in December 1995. It was published in full in *An Sionnach* (USA).

All quotations from Van Morrison are courtesy of Van Morrison, Exile Productions and Faber & Faber, publishers of *Lit Up Inside: Selected Lyrics*, to whom thanks and kind acknowledgements are also made.

SELECT BIBLIOGRAPHY

Bardon, Jonathan, *Belfast: An Illustrated History* (Belfast: Blackstaff Press, 1982).

Boyd, John, Archive, Linenhall Library, Belfast.

Bell, Sam Hanna, *The Hollow Ball* (London: Cassell, 1961).

Bort, Eberhord, *Commemorating Ireland: History, Politics, Culture* (Dublin: Irish Academic Press, 2004).

Brown, Terence, 'Let's Go to Graceland: The Drama of Stewart Parker' in Nicholas Allen and Aaron Kelly (eds), *The Cities of Belfast* (Dublin: Four Courts Press, 2003), pp. 117–26.

Bruce, Steve, *God Save Ulster* (Oxford: Clarendon Press, 1986).

—, *The Edge of the Union* (Oxford: Oxford University Press, 1994).

Buckland, Patrick, *A History of Northern Ireland* (Dublin: Gill and Macmillan, 1981).

Charters, Anne, *The Penguin Book of the Beats* (Harmondsworth: Penguin, 1993).

Clarkson, Leslie, 'The City and the Country' in *Belfast: The Making of the City 1800–1914* (Belfast: Appletree Press, 1983).

Collins, Brenda, 'The Edwardian City' in *Belfast: The Making of the City 1800–1914* (Belfast: Appletree Press, 1983).

Corcoran, Mary P. & Peillon, Michel, *Uncertain Ireland: A Sociological Chronicle, 2003–2004* (Dublin: Institute of Public Administration, 2006).

Craig, Patricia (ed.), *The Belfast Anthology* (Belfast: Blackstaff Press, 1999).

De Brún, Fionntán, *Belfast and the Irish Language* (Dublin: Four Courts Press, 2006).

Durcan, Paul, 'The Drumshambo Hustler: A Celebration of Van Morrison', *Magill* (May 1988).

Foster, John Wilson, 'A Belfast Childhood', *Irish Literary Supplement* (Autumn 1989).

—, *The Titanic Complex: A Cultural Manifest* (Belfast: Belcouver Press, 1997).

Grimble, Ian, *Scottish Clans and Tartans* (London: Hamlyn, 1973).

Johnstone, Robert, 'Stewart Parker: 1941–1988', *Honest Ulsterman*, No. 86, Spring/Summer 1989.

Kavanagh, Patrick, 'Poetry Since Yeats: An Exchange of Views', *Tri-Quarterly*, No. 4, 1965.

—, *Selected Poems* (ed. Antoinette Quinn) (London: Penguin Books, 2000).

Keats, John, *The Letters* (ed. F. Page) (Oxford: Oxford University Press, 1954).

Kerouac, Jack, *On the Road* (Harmondsworth: Penguin, 1972 [1957]).

Larkin, Philip, *All What Jazz: A Record Diary 1961–1971* (London: Faber and Faber, 1985).

Mac Mathúna, Ciarán, *Traditional Music: Whose*

Music? in Peter MacNamee (ed.) (Belfast: Institute of Irish Studies, 1991).

McKay, Patrick, *Belfast Place-names and the Irish Language* (Dublin: Four Courts Press, 2006).

MacNeice, Louis, *Collected Poems* (ed. Peter McDonald) (London: Faber & Faber, 2010).

Maguire, W.A., *Belfast* (Lancaster: Carnegie Publishing, 2009 [1993]).

Melly, George, *Revolt into Style: The Pop Arts* (Oxford: Oxford University Press, 1989).

Morrison, Van, *Lit Up Inside: Selected Lyrics* (London: Faber & Faber, 2014).

—, *Coney Island of the Mind* documentary.

Parker, Stewart, *Three Plays for Ireland: Northern Star; Heavenly Bodies; Pentecost* (London: Oberon Books, 1980).

—, 'Me & Jim', *Irish University Review*, James Joyce Special Issue, 12:1, 1982.

—, 'Dramatis Personae: John Malone Memorial Lecture', *Dramatis Personae & Other Writings*, edited by Gerald Dawe, Maria Johnston and Clare Wallace (New York: Syracuse University Press, 2009).

—, *High Pop, Stewart Parker's Irish Times Column 1970–1976*, edited by Gerald Dawe and Maria Johnston (Belfast: Lagan Press, 2008).

Power, Vincent, *Send 'Em Home Sweatin': The Showband Story* (Dublin: Kildanore Press, 1990).

York, Richie, *Van Morrison: Into the Music* (London: Futura, 1975).